DISPLACED

A HOLOCAUST MEMOIR AND THE ROAD TO A NEW BEGINNING

LINDA SCHWAB

WITH TODD M. MEALY, PH.D.

SUNBURY PRESS

Mechanicsburg, PA USA

Published by Sunbury Press, Inc.
Mechanicsburg, Pennsylvania

www.sunburypress.com

For information about special discounts for bulk purchases, please contact Sunbury Press Orders Dept. at (855) 338-8359 or orders@sunburypress.com.

To request one of our authors for speaking engagements or book signings, please contact Sunbury Press Publicity Dept. at publicity@sunburypress.com.

ISBN: 978-1-62006-386-6 (Trade paperback)

Library of Congress Control Number: 2019957722

FIRST SUNBURY PRESS EDITION: January 2020

Product of the United States of America
0 1 1 2 3 5 8 13 21 34 55

Set in Adobe Garamond
Designed by Crystal Devine
Cover by Lawrence Knorr
Edited by Lawrence Knorr

Continue the Enlightenment!

To my father, Hendel Svidler.

— Linda Schwab

My work on this book is dedicated to Linda Schwab, whose story is an inspiration for countless people around the world. This is also in memory of my grandfathers, Eugene Mealy and James Marafioti. They were among millions of men who fought bravely and honorably against the Nazis during World War II.

— Todd M. Mealy

INTRODUCTION

WHAT IS IT that makes Holocaust stories so compelling? Books on the topic are popular among middle schoolers as much as they are among the middle-aged. Still, in 2020, the list of scholarly works on Jewish studies as well as the Final Solution and Holocaust memoirs written by survivors continues to grow. *The Crime and the Silence: Confronting the Massacre of Jews in Wartime Jedwabne* (2015) by Anna Bikont won the 2015 National Jewish Book Award for its content surrounding the massive pogrom in Jedwabne, Poland on July 10, 1941. Peter Hayes provides a revisionist approach to the contours of Holocaust studies in *Why? Explaining the Holocaust* (2017). Of course, much of Hayes' work was published in the wake of the foremost scholar on Holocaust studies, Timothy Snyder. Among Snyder's most noteworthy work is *The New York Times* bestseller and Editors' Choice award-winning *Black Earth: The Holocaust as History and Warning* (2015). It would be a grave error if I fail to mention several memoirs that fall within the literary canon of Holocaust scholarship—yes, I called the black sheep of literature—memoirs—scholarship. Holocaust memoirs like Chil Rajchman's *The Last Jew of Treblinka* have shaped public consciousness as much as, if not more than, slave narratives. Eli Weisel's *Night,* Helene Berr's *The Journal of Helene Berr* and *The Diary of Anne Frank* affects readers in profound ways, just as *Twelve Years a Slave, Narrative of the Life of Frederick Douglass, an American Slave,* and

Incidents in the Life of a Slave Girl. What do slave narratives, Holocaust memoirs, and academic books on the topic have in common? They all document suffering and redemption.

Years ago, Daniel Mendelsohn claimed this suffering-and-redemptive narrative had "universality." Mendlesohn suggested that readers "bear an awful burden" as much as Holocaust writers and Holocaust survivors. Why, then, does the Holocaust genre far outweigh its literary rivals? The answer, perhaps, is that nearly everyone goes through their own anguish and torment. Readers, in other words, suffer through their own holocaust.

Linda Schwab's Holocaust memoir, *Displaced: A Memoir of a Holocaust Survivor and the Road to a New Beginning*, speaks not necessarily from a historically suppressed lens, but of a messy, hybridized, cultural manifestation in Eastern Europe that changed hands continuously during her childhood. Whether suppressed by the Soviets or the Nazis, Schwab and her Jewish neighbors were forced to live as a subclass with limited chances at freedom, social mobility, or the development and redevelopment of a culture. In *Displaced*, Schwab uses the complicated Polish-Belarusian border as a way to explain her existence as a racialized "Other" in Eastern Europe. Schwab and her Jewish neighbors were alienated in her Myadel *shtetl* just as racialized groups have been in the United States. As she evaded the Nazis for nearly two years in Poland's Ponar Forest only to escape to the United States with her parents and two brothers in 1949, she learned that limitations to her cultural identity were not restricted to Eastern Europe.

Upon her relocation across the Atlantic Ocean with the help of President Truman's Displaced Persons Act, Schwab spent most of her formative years grappling with her linguistic, spiritual, and ideological identity, which blurred at times as she observed the struggles of the civil rights movement on television. She also repressed her emotions at times when trying to prove herself a loyal American during the infamous McCarthy witch hunts of the 1950s.

During the winter of 1942, Schwab and her two brothers, Chaim Zelman and Nochum, watched their parents dig a cave in the Ponar Forest outside of present-day Myadel, Belarus, where they hid from the *SS* and Polish collaborators for 18 months. It has been about 75 years since she left that cave. Three children and a gang of grandchildren later, not a day has gone by that she hasn't been haunted by the memory of what happened to her family. Schwab has also spent much of her life suffering from survivor's guilt, knowing that millions had lost their lives in Nazi killing centers. She was able to avoid being sent to a death camp because of the brave and heroic acts of her parents and a few compassionate neighbors.

The time is right to read Linda Schwab's memoir now that a 2018 poll conducted by the Conference on Jewish Material Claims Against Germany revealed that 70 percent of Americans say fewer people seem to care about the Holocaust than ever before. Strikingly, 11 percent of adults and 22 percent of Millennials "haven't heard" or "are not sure if they have heard of the Holocaust." Despite the fact that approximately six million Jews, seven million Soviet civilians, nearly two million non-Jewish Poles, and 200,000 Roma and Sinti died at the hands of the Nazis, which includes the loss of 1.5 million children, nearly 31 percent of all Americans and over 41 percent of Millennials believe that "two million Jews or less were killed during the Holocaust."[1] The poll indicated that those who had heard of the Holocaust assumed that its genocide was restricted to Germany. Reality is, almost 90 percent of the Jewish population living in the Baltic States was killed. The survey also reported that just 45 percent of adults and about half (49 percent) of Millennials could not name one of the 1,300 concentration camps and ghettos in Europe during the Third Reich's reign. At a rate of 66 percent, the study states, Millennials could not identify Auschwitz, the largest and deadliest death camp in Poland.[2]

The survey contains implications that are troubling for anti-racist activists and Holocaust survivors like Linda Schwab. There are visible signals of a racially divided United States. The critical gaps, the survey illuminates, "both in awareness of basic facts and detailed knowledge

---

1. Andre Pitzer. *One Long Night: A Global History of Concentration Camps.* (Boston: Little, Brown and Company, 2017)

2. Claims Conference. "New Survey by Claims Conference Finds Significance Knowledge in the United States." *The Conference on Jewish material Claims Against Germany.* February 2018. *http://www .claimscon.org/study*

of the Holocaust" suggest that something like a Holocaust can happen again.[3] Indeed, between 2017 and 2019, verbal and deadly attacks against Jews and other racial, religious, and gender minorities in the United States have occurred in places like Charlottesville, Pittsburgh, and San Diego. This is not to ignore mass violence across the world in the last three decades: an estimated 800,000 Tutsis killed in Rwanda in 1994, 7,000 Bosnian Muslims at Srebrenica in 1995, 300,000 in Darfur between 2003 and 2013, and the death and displacement of several thousand Rohingya Muslims in Myanmar since 2016.[4] Schwab, who has expressed the purpose of her memoir to be "so people don't forget," has genuine concern about educators shirking their duty to teach evidentiary truths about the Holocaust. Her resolve is so real, she has given scholarships to deserving students from her hometown of Harrisburg, Pennsylvania to go on the annual International March of the Living, a program that brings individuals from around the world to Poland and Israel to learn about the Holocaust and, according to the organization, to "examine the roots of prejudice, intolerance, and hatred."[5]

Linda Schwab's life has been about more than defeating racism and bigotry, but a constant theme that runs through this memoir is her desire to conquer indifference. To live as a bystander to injustice is morally wrong. Through this book and her public speaking, it has become Schwab's personal mission to confront anti-Semitism and fight back against hatred toward any group of people. Small acts of hate matter, writes Andrea Pitzer, author of *One Long Night: A Global History of Concentration Camps*. They add up. Especially when powerful institutions commit them. Left unchecked, Pitzer adds, hatred grows worse. Bad intentions are not required from the people charged with governing citizens for harm to result. As seen in the gradual progression of the Holocaust from laws to ghettos to labor camps to mobile death squads

3. Claims Conference. "New Survey by Claims Conference Finds Significance Knowledge in the United States." *The Conference on Jewish material Claims Against Germany.* February 2018. *http://www.claimscon.org/study*

4. Paul Behrens, Olaf Jenen, Nicholas Terry. *Holocaust and Genocide Denial: A Contextual Perspective.* (New York: Taylor & Francis, May 18, 2017) 1; Anders Hastrup. *The War in Darfur: Reclaiming Sudanese History* (New York: Routledge, 2013)

5. Ibid.

to systematic killing centers over the span of twelve years between 1933 and 1945, policy and public indifference will be enough to result in terrorizing marginalized communities: vis-à-vis, preemptively detaining immigrants of Eastern European origin without trial after the Great War, the internment of Japanese-American during World War II, and the existence of "tent cities" and "tender age" centers for asylum-seeking children come to mind.

High school and college students are often surprised to hear there is a growing Holocaust denial movement. Denial of this genocide is rooted in distorting everything we know about the Holocaust. This repulsive yet prevailing movement began in 1959 when *Mein Kampf* reading neo-Nazi George Lincoln Rockwell, also known as the "American Fuhrer" and founder of the American Nazi Party, launched a fake news campaign to discredit stories about the Holocaust. Using the pseudonym Lew Cor, Rockwell made up stories that Cor supposedly had witnessed during the war. Rockwell then sold his sham stories to the men's pulp magazine *Sir!*. As noted by Vegas Tenold in *Everything You Love Will Burn*, Rockwell's plan was to plant fake accounts of Nazi death camps as a way to say the Holocaust was a hoax: "This one is all lies, and I should know because I made it up," Tenold explains Rockwell's motives. Thereafter, all other stories about Nazi atrocities would be tainted with doubt. "If one story was fake," Tenold adds, "wasn't there a chance all of them were?"[6]

Despite the abundance of documents and memoirs, historian Deborah E. Lipstadt writes, the Holocaust has been dismissed by some as "contrived," "coerced," and "forgeries and falsehoods."[7] Schwab's solution to this reprehensible attack on the truth is for the few remaining survivors to go "on record." Lipstadt attests to this assertion in her book *Denying the Holocaust: The Growing Assault on Truth and Memory*. As fewer survivors remain with us that can personally challenge those

6. Vegas Tenold. *Everything You Love Will Burn: Inside the Rebirth of White Nationalism in America* (New York: Nation Books, 2017), 105-7; William H. Scmaltz. *For Race and Nation: George Lincoln Rockwell and the American Nazi Party* (River's Bend Press, 2013)

7. Deborah E. Lipstadt. *Denying the Holocaust: The Growing Assault on Truth and Memory* (New York: Simon and Schuster, 2012).

shameful attacks, Lipstadt suggests, the deniers "will only grow in intensity."[8] The numbers previously mentioned by the Conference on Jewish Material Claims Against Germany indicate the impact that Holocaust denial has had on the public consciousness. Schwab reinforces this point in the opening statement of her public speaking events: "There aren't many of us left," she often says, "and because I survived, I feel I have to tell my story."

When hatred is allowed to proceed unchecked, it can become the status quo. In America, Jim Crow segregation and popular culture symbols of hatred reigned supreme decades before and after Schwab's arrival to America. For years, many questioned whether the United States' segregation laws had something to do with Nazi efforts to oppress Europe's Jewish population. James Q. Whitman settled the question in 2017. In his book, *Hitler's American Model: The United States and the Making of Nazi Race Law*, Whitman describes in detail how Franz Gurtner, the Third Reich's Minister of Justice, and other Nazi legal authorities mined America's Jim Crow laws "for inspiration during the making of the Nuremberg Laws."[9] Hitler, himself, praised the United States in *Mein Kampf* as "the one state"[10] that provided a template for establishing a caste system that divided people along racial lines.

If not the work of scholars, Linda Schwab's memoir will remind us how hatred develops. It will make us ponder ways to confront it. We are urged to remember that the Holocaust happened: to remember that ordinary human beings are capable of perpetrating harm. In the end, Schwab calls on us all to care about injustice, even when we are not the targets of injustice, and to look beyond our own lives so that no one ever again has to be displaced by hatred.

Todd M. Mealy, Ph.D.

Lancaster, Pennsylvania
2020

8. Ibid.
9. James Q. Whitman. *Hitler's American Model: The United States and the Making of Nazi Race Law.* (Princeton University Press, 2017).
10. Quoted in Whitman.

CHAPTER 1

IT IS VERY difficult for me to talk about my childhood because I never had one.

My earliest memories are painful, absent of the joy and innocence that comes with being a rambunctious kid. My thoughts take me inside my house in Myadel. Beyond those walls, I can only remember Nazi soldiers taking over my *shtetl*, or village, in Poland.

I know that my family lived in a bustling part of Myadel. Surely, only a few of the streets were cobblestone. Certainly, the village square, where my home rested, had to be narrow. A combination of bicycles and horse-drawn carriages were the main means of transportation in and out of town. This simple lifestyle made Myadel a quaint locale, but also culturally rich.

I cannot remember what I did for fun before the war. Our *shtetl* had at its western edge a lake. Lake Narach, I do recall. My cousins from Vilna used to tell me that we spent summers and holidays at the lake. But I do not remember. I am sure I played there with my two brothers, Chaim Zelman and Nochum, in the summertime. I can imagine my family spent plenty of warm, sunny, and cloudless days along the bank of the lake. I would bet that my older brother, Chaim Zelman, splashed in its clear blue and calming ripples. But these kinds of childhood memories fail me. Today there are lovely hills that loom in a blue haze throughout the Narach region. The pasture has always teemed with fishermen, deer, elk, otter, and muskrats. I am convinced that it had to be just as beautiful an area during my childhood as it is today.

What I do recollect is that my *shtetl* sat within the eastern region of the Vilna province, in an area that used to be part of Poland between the two world wars. Today, Myadel is in Belarus. There was a train station in town that would take passengers all over the area. Vilna, with its complex history of being passed back and forth between Polish and Lithuanian-Soviet government officials, was always the center of activity for people in my area of Poland. It rested just 120 kilometers west of my village.

My father, Hendel Svidler, always an astute individual, was born the youngest of 17 children in Svintzan, near Vilna. His father, Chaim (my brother's namesake), died when my father was very young. My father and all of his siblings were left in the care of my father's mother—my amazing grandmother—Glila Scaplovich. The people in their village called her "Glila de Chachoma," meaning "Brilliant." Not only did she raise her 17 children by herself, folks in town always came to her for help. She was the sage of Svintzan.

Life before the war didn't come hard for my father, whom we called "Pop." He was bright and always so pleasant to people. His knowledge and wisdom of the Torah were remarkable. He could recite much of the *Siddur* and *Machzor* prayers by heart. The *Siddur* is the Jewish prayer book containing three daily prayers as well as the prayers for the *Shabbat*, *Rosh-Chodesh*, and the Three Festivals (Passover, Shavuot, and Sukkot). The *Machzor* contains the prayers for *Rosh Hashanah* and *Yom Kippur*. Pop's aptitude for the Torah was the reason why my parents were married.

It is common in Jewish custom for marriages to be arranged. I have trouble, however, using that term to describe my parents' union. They never spoke of their nuptials as having been arranged. While a *shadchan*, or matchmaker, paired them when they were in their mid-twenties, theirs' was a special relationship. For reasons that are difficult to explain, my parents' families allowed my mother and father to date for a period before their nuptials. Following a loving courtship, my parents were married in 1927. The *shadchan* was impressed with my father's knowledge of the Torah. Consequently, that is why he was introduced to my mother, Reva, the daughter of one of the chief rabbis of Vilna, Anshul Aronovitch.

The Aronovitches were *Lubavitch* or Orthodox Jews. As one of the chief *Lubavitch* rabbis in the city, Rebbe Anshul provided strength and spiritual leadership to the Jewish community. He oversaw a Jewish printing factory called Rhoms Druckerie. Every religious book was manufactured and signed by him. When a rabbi from a certain *beit telifah*, house of prayer, had a problem solving community problems, they would come before the board of rabbis for a decision. My maternal grandfather headed the board of rabbis.

Long considered the epicenter of Jewish creativity and political life, Vilna had one of the largest Jewish populations in Eastern Europe. Some 30 synagogues provided spiritual refuge for the 60,000 Jews that lived in the city. Everyone called it "Little Jerusalem," as more Jews lived there than in Palestine at the time. The language of the Jewish population in Vilna was predominantly Yiddish. Most residents worked jobs in industry and craft, but our people were left in a state of economic despair after World War I. Polish nationals branded Jews "enemies" and shortly after my parents were married, about the same time that the Nazis took power in Germany, a number of violent clashes led to the death of Jews in Vilna and property was destroyed. This is why, after the wedding at my grandfather's synagogue in Vilna, my parents chose to relocate from a small, overcrowded house to the village of Myadel on Lake Narach.

Although he was so religious, my grandfather was also very open-minded. In defiance of the standard gender norms of that era, he sent his five daughters to Vilnius University. His family also belonged to the *Maccabi*, a sports association in Vilna that allowed my mother to play tennis. To participate in sports and to attend the university were both considered unusual for women at the time. I think my mother had five sisters. I remember four of them (Ida, Sonia, Dina, Rocheland), but not the fifth.

Pop brought his four sisters, Basia, Henya, Belike, and Eda, with him. It was a resort town, owing much to the pleasant surroundings of the lake and rather close proximity to the hustle and bustle of Vilna. Most of the Jewish population in Myadel was in the retail business. They were tailors, shoemakers, candy salesmen, bicycle shop owners, Kosher butchers, and bakers. My dad earned plenty of money as a fabric merchant, livestock rancher, and owner of an orchard. By the time my brothers and I were born, he was able to purchase a relatively large red brick house in the village's square.

Behind our new home was a large vegetable garden. On one side of the house was a barn with horses and cows. We would make our own cheese, butter, and milk. We also had our own chickens. In accordance with *kaparot* ritual, we would always slaughter a chicken for *Shabbat* or the Jewish Sabbath. Pop was very generous to our neighbors. He would often give away food when they were in need.

When I was young, my father built an attachment to our house. He moved his fabric store there. Ready-made clothing was not available then. The fabric had to be purchased by the villagers to sell at home. He would travel to Vilna to purchase the material wholesale. As a result, he had the largest and best selection in Myadel. The combination of the fabric shop with our back-yard garden and livestock farm, suddenly Pop's store became one-stop shopping for everyone in the village. His reputation throughout the Vilnius region had grown exponentially before I was born. Nearly everyone, rich and poor, would come to him for their day-to-day needs. My father was very friendly with his patrons, especially his recurring customers, whom he considered his friends. Whenever a needy person visited the shop—Jew and Gentile, alike—Pop would let them go to the back and take what they needed. When customers did not have the money to pay immediately, he would accept written records of debt. "My customers were my friends," he always said. Pop saw the best in people and never expressed reservations about believing that his customers would pay at a later date.

My father once told us about a family—a father with six sons. They were all priests without any money. They would come to my father just to visit and talk. Another friend, an Arab, or Lipka Tartar, would come and visit with him. Pop gave them all food, and they were truly his friends. "Arabs were citizens of Poland too," Pop said. "They had no one to talk to so they would come and talk to me."

The people valued Pop for the level of companionship he offered others. The way my father ran his business ended up being the reason why we were able to survive the Holocaust. Both Jews and Gentiles were important for our survival when we went into hiding, as you will see in chapters 8 and 9.

In those days, the government would not allow Jews to own farms. So my father purchased two orchards outside of town. He would visit them every week on his bicycle, as there were no cars and it was faster than going by horse and buggy.

The village itself was predominately made up of Jews. There were two synagogues in Myadel. The largest in the village was located on our street, *Yiddisha Gas*, or Jewish Street. In general, the Jews in Myadel lived happy lives. Jewish families were able to raise their children by going to *chedar*, or school, to study the Jewish religion. Oh, how I looked forward to going to school. My parents made all the right decisions for my brothers and me. But then war clouds rolled in. Following behind were the Germans.

CHAPTER 2

I ENTERED THIS world as Glila Svidler on the fifth day of *Hanukkah*, December 25, 1935. I was named after my wonderful paternal grandmother. Everyone called me "Lile."

My parents told me that I was "born in the sac." Being born with a caul or the amniotic membrane is taken as a sign of good luck, which is a *bobe mayse*; it means a grandmother's tale. I have always taken pride in being compared to Jacob, the "heel grabber" as the scripture says. My Pop, the Biblical scholar, said I was like Jacob, a twin son born to Isaac and Rebecca, grandson of Abraham and Sarah. Like Jacob, they called me the "lucky one" who, I was told, was likewise, "born in the sac." My father always told me I was strong like Jacob, that I was a fighter.

A midwife in the home where I grew up delivered me. In fact, all of us children had our own midwife and our own nanny. My nanny's name was Paluta. She took care of me when my parents worked in my father's fabric store. Paluta had an easy time with me since I was so young. On the other hand, my older brother's nanny had to chase him around much of the time as he unceasingly engaged in adolescent behavior that could have caused serious injury to his body. He hopped on the furniture and played rough sports. To his credit, Chaim was always very athletic. He inherited his athleticism from our mother, who was a remarkable tennis player. Since he was two years older than me before the war broke out, Chaim had plenty of opportunities to develop his athletic skills, especially soccer. He was a talented soccer player.

Though our village of Myadel was located in independent Poland, we were considered Litvaks, or Lithuanian Jews. Most of the Jews in our *shtetl* were Litvaks. There were about 70 Jewish families in our village. We all lived typical religious-based Jewish lives. Jewish children were raised to go to *chedar* to study the Jewish religion in one of the two synagogues. There was one called Myadel Nowy located on *Yiddisha Gas* and the other situated a few blocks north of our home called Yenne Myadel, known to everyone in the village as "the other Myadel." *Chedar* was sometimes held in private homes. The spiritual leader of our *shtetl* was a friend of my mother and father, Rabbi Avraham Shmuel Kosczevsky. Rabbi Koszcevsky was a legend in town. He was from an area of the Russian Empire called Eisiskes (later independent Poland, but now Lithuania), where he taught at *Yesheva* or college. During World War I, he was separated from his wife and six children for four years. After the war, he tracked down his family in Zaremby Koszceine, a town in newly independent Poland. They moved to Myadel in 1933.

For as much education that my father possessed, and regardless of how many personal connections he had with important people in the region, he held little curiosity about politics. He never described himself as Zionist. Neither did my mother. They were devoted to their business and us children. My brothers and I paid no attention to the expansion of the Third Reich in areas of Eastern Europe. Why would we? We were young. And our parents saw no reason to panic when Adolf Hitler and Joseph Stalin signed the German-Soviet Pact in the summer of 1939.

On September 1, 1939, however, the Germans invaded the Prussian area of Poland. Two weeks later, on September 17, Soviet soldiers attacked our country from the East. Both nations claimed territory that once belonged to their then-dissolved empires.

There was little Polish resistance to the Red Army. Many of us were under the impression that the Russians were there to protect us from the Nazis, who had years earlier effectively declared Jews a racial adversary that needed to be handled. In a clear no-win situation, Jews were more accepting of the Soviets, who looked at us only as class foes that could be dealt with nonviolently. And in fact, we were. Polish and Jewish citizens throughout Soviet-occupied Poland had land and businesses liquidated by the Soviet soldiers.

We experienced this refined terror directly. Once the Russians were firmly established in Myadel, they had my father and all the wholesalers keep stores open until they sold out of their merchandise. Even though Soviet rubles were worthless, Pop was forced to accept it as recompense for his goods. Once he ran out of inventory, the store and our property were seized by the Soviets. Our home had become a collectivized farm used to fulfill Moscow-imposed quotas. My father, whose prized reputation across the region caught the Soviets' attention, was given two State jobs: one as a veterinarian and the other as a sap collector for a company called Reicheem Leshoseh. We were fortunate that he was given employment in a profession other than the peasantry. This particular job maintained my father's status as a leading figure among the people in Myadel.

This was certainly better than the fate Jewish communities experienced elsewhere in Eastern Europe. Indeed, the resultant "class struggle" of having businesses liquidated and properties confiscated in Soviet-occupied Poland created great financial strain to the people in Myadel, Jewish and Gentile alike. On the other hand, however, there was either the German genocide of the west or the Soviet counter-revolutionary programs of the east.

Our relatives in Soviet-controlled Vilna were among those less fortunate. On June 15, the Red Army's tanks rolled into Vilna. The total Soviet occupation of the Baltic States had begun. The overwhelming presence of a large affluent Jewish population that possessed political influence in the region frightened the Soviets. Always concerned about a potential fifth column conspiracy that could awaken a rebellion and incessant consciousness about former World War I-era soldiers and anti-Soviet activists that had once fought against the Russian Empire, the

Soviet occupiers treated every man, woman, and child in Vilnius with contempt. Though there was no planned genocide like the German had already commenced in Prussia, the Russian soldiers in Vilna treated private farmers, teachers, and intellectuals—and their families—as class enemies. Many were arrested, deported, and murdered.

After the Soviet soldiers had enough time to pillage the city for spoils, a speedy governmental transition of power occurred when the Russians ceded the Vilnius region to the newly created state of Lithuania. By 1940, Vilna was no longer part of Poland. An international border between Myadel and Vilna now separated us from my cousins.

Though it may sound peculiar since our village was surrounded by such ugliness and cruelty, my life was unnoticeably interrupted that first year. News about Jewish refugees escaping the Nazi-occupied regions of West Poland filtered into my home as my parents received letters from relatives living in Vilna, where Prussia's Jewish refugees had escaped. More stories were shared at my Pop's fabric store before it was closed. Freedom fighters in Vilna put out a call encouraging Jews to stream into that city for safety. Some people from Myadel answered the call and moved to Vilna, where they thought it would be safer in the long run. Instead of leaving, Pop buried much of our gold deep into the ground next to a tree in our backyard. We then continued on with our comparatively normal lives. My parents made the decision to stay put.

Was this the right decision? Would life under Soviet occupation grow more dreadful? Or would the Nazis arrive to ravage more territory in Poland? If so, what would become of our fate? How would my Jacob-like luck get me through these confusing times?

CHAPTER 3

THE MOOD CHANGED in January 1940 when Lithuanian security forces tightened the border between Poland and Lithuania. No longer were Jewish refugees accepted into the region. As for those expatriates already in Vilna, Lithuanian military officials told them to leave the city. Only those who could prove that they lived in Vilna before 1919—in the former Russian empire—were given Lithuanian citizenship. This regulation banished more than just Jews. It forced Gentile Poles to evacuate the country too. By springtime, all of Lithuania had been annexed by the Soviet Union. Lithuania was now a Soviet Socialist Republic.

It was during this time that letters from my grandparents and cousins who lived in Vilna stopped coming. Lithuanian nationals started working with the Soviet soldiers to restrict the religious rights of Jews. Polish people, Jews and Gentiles, were persecuted by the Soviet-Lithuanian military order. Lithuanian nationals had free reign to terrorize Galician Jews (Polish Jews) and Jewish Litvaks like my relatives.

Mom had just given birth to my younger brother, Nochum. So this was a time I started asking questions about what was happening in Vilna. I wanted to repress any news that my family might have been harmed. I did not want to think that this would happen in my *shtetl*. Thinking that if I stayed indoors and out of trouble, the bad guys would overlook my village. I refused to leave the house. My older brother, Chaim Zelman, made jokes and wandered through the neighborhood playing with his friends. For a year, I helped Mom with Nochum and never thought about what was happening to our relatives. Mom and Pop would remind me that I was a child and that I needed to play like children play. "Look, Lile," Mom would say to me, "Go out and play with Chaim Zelman." I listened and then murmured something back to her. I usually just went to my room to be alone.

When winter turned to spring, and as the snow melted, dead bodies were discovered in the forest between Myadel and Vilna. Pop explained to us that the bodies were of those that tried to relocate to Vilna the previous year. They had been kept out by Soviet and Lithuanian border security, where they froze in the woods. He did not tell us that they had been shot. Chaim Zelman and I sat in stunned silence, staring at one another. We were young. But word about the fate that had befallen Jews like us was just too much to cope with. Luckily, Nochum was too young to realize what was going on in the world. And our resilient parents never showed cracks of anxiousness or fragility during this trying time.

"I don't believe there is anything to worry about," Mom reassured with a smile. "Chaim Zelman, you, and Nochum are all safe."

Mom's assurances were convincing, especially as spring became summer. Then summer turned to fall. The new year arrived without any violence in Myadel.

Everyone in my family went through their daily routines. From sunup to sundown, Pop did his sap work. Sometimes my mother would help him. Other times she was preoccupied with my baby brother. I spent my days with Paluta, my nanny. Chaim Zelman played soccer with his friends from the village. It was springtime in 1941. Almost two years had gone by since the war began, and our small village was still unaffected by the war.

Things would change soon, nonetheless.

CHAPTER 4

THOSE THAT REMAINED in Myadel during the period of Soviet occupation had the same naïve thoughts as my parents. They remained in denial that the Nazis were inflicting unspeakable atrocities on the people of West Poland. Whether nostalgic myth or just sense-lessness, my parents recalled the *Deutsche Heer*, or German Army, that peaceably occupied this territory during World War I. On no occasion before 1941 had the German occupying forces in the West threatened the lives of neither my family nor my relatives in Vilna. Other Litvaks scattered in Lithuanian and Belarusian territories were also unharmed by the Germans. Thinking optimistically, my parents and likeminded Jews that had once owned properties and businesses in our village thought it best to remain at home. Pop and Mom were hard-working, well-to-do, and positive individuals that once had many personal and financial investments in Myadel before the Soviets arrived. They were optimistic about the future. Would we get back our orchards and garden? What would happen to our home? It might sound morose because there was no benign German rule anywhere in Europe, but I truly feel that their decision to remain at home was the right decision at the time. I know now that we likely would not have survived had we gone to stay with family in Vilna.

I remember vividly the day that marked the beginning of the end of peace in Myadel. How do I forget the *Kubelwagens*, the German jeeps? How could I not still picture the Nazi soldiers on their motorcycles with sidecars? The images of well-dressed soldiers, brandishing whips with dogs from their K-9 units at their sides, and their rifles suspended over their shoulders were seared into my brain. How can I ever forget the sound of Nazi calf-high jackboots tramping tempestuously along the cobblestone outside of my house?

The danger that befell to my family and all of the Jews in Myadel began on June 21, 1941, the day that the Germans broke its truce with the Soviets by crossing the Vistula and Bug rivers in route to invading Eastern Poland. German *Wehrmacht* troops took the Soviet defense by surprise. The Red Army suffered disastrous losses in Vilnius, which made it easy for the *Einsatzgruppen,* or *Schutzstaffel (SS),* to enter into the region in the wake of the troops.

The arrival of the Germans troops meant the departure of the Russians. It also meant the beginning of the "Aryanization," or forced exclusion of Jews from society, of this part of Poland, as Jews were almost immediately denaturalized, resulting in the transfer of Jewish land and other assets to the control of non-Jews. Jews, moreover, were soon excluded from Polish cultural institutions, universities, and most of the integral occupations in the community that included doctors, lawyers, and bankers. Many of the Jews, in particular, retreated with the Russians. Most, we learned, ended up in Siberia. My father chose not to follow because my siblings and I were too young. This was a courageous decision despite the rumors that the Germans were killing Polish Jews.

The siege on my *shtetl* began in July when two patrol cars carrying four *Wehrmacht* soldiers apiece arrived in the square around supper-time. The occupation force didn't grow much larger than that since we were a small community, but our tiny *shtetl* was taken quite easily. We were all stunned. While rumors of the war's escalation had reached us, the people in Myadel were neither armed nor ready to defend one another. No one was willing to challenge the German troops. What good would have come from that anyway? In fact, while my family and our Jewish neighbors watched the Nazi soldiers with dread, many of the Polish nationals around our village greeted the occupiers with cheers. The bewildering thing was to see how many men and women went along with them. It was sickening to see the silence and complicity by many of our neighbors, many of who had shopped in my Pop's retail store for years. The Germans appointed some of the nationals to take command of the police force. At the head of the police was a *Burgermeister*, or town master, named Baginisky.

As the sunset, and into the next morning, Baginisky and some of his thuggish collaborators helped the Nazis identify all of the Jews in the village. It was not that difficult of a task. As the soldiers were guided around the village, the nationals would simply point out the *mezuzah* on the doorposts of all the Jewish houses. First, there would be a loud knock at the door. Then, without inflicting any physical pain on anyone in those early hours of the occupation, the German soldiers filled out a registry of the names and addresses of all the Jewish people in the *shtetl*.

Our village was not large enough to be substantially transformed like Vilna, Warsaw, or even Amsterdam. And yet, our lives were turned over at rapid speed as the arrival of the Nazis changed everything for our family and everything about our village. As the days progressed, the farmers could sell their food only through the Germans and Polish nationals. Movement of food and other inventory across the village was not permitted without approval, which usually resulted in pillaging by the occupying forces instead of legal commercial transactions. Baginisky allowed my father to retain his job as the village veterinarian. He knew that Pop owned livestock. Pop would prove his value only days later when disease spread among the cattle in Myadel. Pop was tasked with solving the crisis. My father's solution was not sophisticated. He collected enough food and water to bathe and feed the cows. He simply revived them. He once told me, "I was like all of the doctors, just a tad bit smarter."

Baginsky would eventually take much joy in allowing the village's Jews to be tormented in ways large and small. There were threats in the streets. Sometimes rocks were thrown through windows. When Pop was gone on his daily business for Baginisky, the Germans and Polish often showed up to pillage our house, including the vegetable garden and cattle we had in the back yard. The same was done to the Jewish-owned stores and Jewish households all over Myadel. The soldiers would sometimes park their vehicles by the roadside and have their lunches in any open space. They would taunt Jewish people that dared to walk near where they congregated. I couldn't believe my eyes. Even today, I ask myself, "Did I actually see this, or did I dream it?"

The arrival of the *Einsatzgruppen* in the shadow of the *Wehrmacht* soldiers was pure terror. Chosen for its loyalty to Hitler during the *Fuhrer's* rise to power a decade earlier, the *SS* death squads were given orders to clean out all potential dangers to the Nazis' war aims, including the plan of turning Poland into a German ethnostate by deporting and eventually annihilating dissenters. This directive gave the *Einsatzgruppen* leeway to pillage and eradicate virtually any group of people they deemed to be potential partisans or saboteurs. Soldiers of the *SS* were especially harsh to Polish resisters because the government never officially surrendered to Germany. The Poles formed an unrelenting underground resistance that inflicted steady acts of damage and disruption against the German occupiers. The German reaction was perceptibly brutal. Poland's Jewish intelligentsia, as well as Jewish political and Jewish cultural elites in Vilnius and Central Russia, were at the top of the list. Men like my father who had no connection to the government or to the Communist Party were targeted by the *Einsatzgruppen* simply because they were military age Jews that might become involved with a resistance force.

At least under Soviet occupation, the children were left alone. Age did not matter with Nazis controlling the streets. Soon after the *SS* subjugated the Jewish people, an involuntary Jewish council known as the *Judenrate* was formed to function as a liaison between the Jewish people of Myadel and the Nazis. This occurred before the construction of any formal ghetto, in part, because most of Myadel's Jews already lived near to one another. Several friends of my Pop's were assigned leadership roles in this community council. They were forced to cooperate with the *SS* by helping to enforce Nazi policy. The *Judenrate* saw that we all complied with newly imposed curfews. It collected personal information about local Jews. At weekly meetings, the Germans gave the *Judenrate* orders to collect assets from the Jewish villagers. Most of the time, the soldiers wanted money. If the committee failed to meet the quota, the Nazis threatened to kill a certain number of us. When the money ran out, the soldiers asked for gold and silver. I remember my mother saying that they wanted us to hand over all of our valuables, including my favorite *Lichter*, or candleholder, that we used for the Sabbath. We all felt that our survival depended on the *Judenrate's* submission to the Nazi overlords.

Never had I heard stories of Pop's or Mom's families having to face the humiliation, or heaven forbid, death in a pogrom. This doesn't mean that their lives were never at risk. Or perhaps the Svidlers and the Scaplovichs were fortunate Jews living in a region of Vilnius sheltered from historical wrongdoings. This existence that I was experiencing, however, was wrought with such foul hatred. I could never have imaged the level of resentment that we all endured during this time. Contempt for the Jews was even reflected by some of our Gentile neighbors. Each passing day brought another Nazi edict that was given to the *Judenrate* and thus levied upon the Jewish people. First, we were barred from entering most public places—schools, parks, restaurants, or post office. Then a curfew was set for 10 o'clock in the evening. We all knew, however, that Jews had to be indoors before sunset. Each decree simply encouraged the Christian people's spiteful behavior toward us. The worst law of all that I remember forced us to sew onto our clothing a canary yellow six-pointed Star of David.

The yellow star decree was enforced pretty quickly after the Nazis first arrived in Myadel. We had to place one badge on the back of our jackets with *Juden* sewn inside the star and another either on our sleeve or chest. Startled, Mom told me, "Don't ask questions; you need to wear this." I had refused to leave the house before this. But now, after this mark of shame was forced upon us, I vowed never to be seen with this thing on my sleeve. I was only six, but my instincts told me that only trouble would be brought upon me if I walked through my village with the six-pointed star on my clothing. So I stayed indoors until demanded by my parents to go play in the backyard. On those few occasions that I walked alongside Pop or Mom, I made sure to brush up close to them as to hide the badge from onlookers.

The yellow star brought humiliation. I can't say it was watching my mother sit in her den sewing the badge onto our clothing that did it, or if it was the glares we would get from our neighbors as if we were criminals, but this was the first time I thought about my religion in a way that separated me from my peers. It made me feel inferior. What had the Jewish people done to deserve such isolation—such dishonor? Why have we lost our Polish citizenship? Why are we no longer treated like human beings?

Pop would share stories of the Middle Ages, when Jews were required to wear a badge in places like England, Sicily, and the Muslim world. These symbols were forced upon the world's Jews to carry out certain social, political, and religious restrictions upon our people. "This method of containment only strengthened our culture," Pop would say as he reassured us that everything would be all right.

Though Pop kept us calm, he concealed his own concern about our future. And it became more difficult to shelter us children from the horrors of what the Germans were doing to the Jewish people in our village. Not long after the *Judenrate* was formed and the yellow star edict was levied upon us did the Germans soldiers, with help from the Polish Police, begin torturing and murdering the Jewish people. My father's sister, Aunt Basia, who worked as a secretary for Burgermeister, was given a note by someone in her office warning her to leave the village. The note read, "The Germans will soon kill you and every other Jew. Get out while you can!"

At first, Pop heeded the warning. He went into the forest, where he once heard that Jews had taken up refuge. There was nowhere to stay. There was no food to eat. "I can't take my children there," he told Mom. So, despite the warning, we stayed.

Then, in August 1941, the military police burned down several Jewish houses. One of the victims was an elderly man named Josef Kotser. After setting the fire, the SS ordered six Jews to go into the still-smoldering house to retrieve Kotser's belongings. As the men exited the home debilitated by smoke exposure, the soldiers unleashed their guard dogs to kill the men.

Each passing day brought more rumors to Myadel. My parents later told me they heard rumors about liquidations taking place through-out Eastern Europe. They heard something tragic had happened in Vilna. By the beginning of September 1941, the Jews of Vilna were placed into two ghettos in the city. My father's family was placed into "Ghetto I," which squeezed in approximately 30,000 Jews. The second ghetto, appropriately called "Ghetto II," was much smaller, detained about 11,000 people. On two occasions during the construction of the ghettoes had the *SS* soldiers conducted *aktions*, or mass executions in secluded locations aiming to kill community leaders, artists, politi-cians, intellectuals, and people suspected of potential anti-Nazi subver-sive activity. The first, so-called "Great Provocation" *aktion*, occurred from August 31 to September 2, resulted in the deaths of some 4,000 Jews, including several members of the Vilna's *Judenrate*. Days later, the Germans forced over 3,000 Jews to strip naked and march single file in groups of twenty to an area of the Vilna forest known as the Ponary. They were told to stand holding hands at the edge of a pit once used by the Soviet Army to store fuel. They were then shot. Their bodies were shoved and kicked into the pit. Dirt was then thrown over their bodies. We heard rumors about German *aktions* in Vilna during that first autumn. By the end of the year, just 20,000 of Vilna's Jews were still alive.

These stories caused my family to grow relatively quiet during the first year of Nazi occupation. My parents had two things on their minds. They both held genuine concerns that this was going to happen to us in Myadel. And two, they believed that my mother's family in

Vilna was dead. Without much warning, near the end of August, my father disappeared, leaving only Mom to take care of us as our nannies left to be with their families. He was gone for days. Where did he go? Why did he go? Was he looking for a place for us to hide? Was he looking into the status of my mother's family? Could he have vanished to the town of his birth, Svintzan, where he had friends? Or was it possible that he fled to one of the *shtetl's* nearby, where he had customers that owed him a debt?

We waited anxiously for our father to return. One day turned to two, then to three. And then I started to think the worst. I worried incessantly about my father's whereabouts. Scenes outside our house looked bleaker every day. And without Mom and Pop together, watching over us, I could only imagine the worst about our fate.

And then, a frightening series of thumps at my door startled me. The Nazis are here.

CHAPTER 5

WE WERE PLACED in the ghetto on August 30, 1941.

Where is Pop? I wondered. *Bang! Bang! Bang!* "Mom!" I sat bolt upright. There was another volley of thuds at the door. *Bang! Bang! Bang!* With Chaim by her side and Nochum in her arms, Mom ran to me. It was then that I realized my mother had all along been scared that we might perish in this war. Where is Pop?

My mother glared at me as she opened the door. "All Jews of Myadel are to be concentrated in a ghetto in another part of the village," commanded the German soldier.

We all looked at one another. The soldier, now impatient, snapped: "Pack a bag. Hurry Up! You won't be moving far away. Let's go!" Mom had no help keeping us calm. Pop was gone. Chaim and I were frozen in that moment. Nochum had tears and snot dripping down his face as he wailed away. We were confused and frightened. We were traumatized by the soldier's aggression. First, the pounding at the door, then with his military police officers standing behind, each with a rifle draped over their shoulders and dogs growling at their sides. The yelling and barking were just too much for us to handle.

Pop! I wondered about my father's whereabouts. My God, will he know where to find us? Or worse, has something bad already happened to him? No one was giving me answers.

"We have to hurry," Mom said as she moved around the house in a frenzy, urging us to get moving. I was hardly helpful as she packed up some clothes and a few of her precious pots and pans. She somehow held the three of us and her packed bag in her two arms as the soldiers escorted us to the ghetto.

The ghetto was small. The Nazis apparently decided that it would be easier for them to monitor us Jews if they packed all of us together into a few houses located on one of Myadel's streets. Almost two hundred Jewish people were crowded into about ten houses of what became Myadel's Jewish Ghetto. Each family, including ours, brought with them a bag of clothing, some porcelain, furniture, and precious heirlooms. I soon learned that holding on to the valuables was not merely for personal safekeeping. It was for the potential use of bartering with the *Judenrate's* demands.

I do not recall how many families were squeezed into the dwelling where we stayed; however, I do remember two of Pop's sisters, Aunt Basia and her husband, Yoshe Leib Yanovsky; as well as Aunt Heiny and her husband, Zalman Kugel, and daughter, Lile, who shared a name with me, were placed with us. We were assigned to share a house that had just a few bedrooms and a tiny kitchen with several families. To make room, we turned bathtubs into beds. Any unnecessary furniture and stoves were removed to create more space. Everyone's belongings, including cots and clothing were thrown everywhere. I shared a bed with my mother and two siblings in one room. It seems like the other families occupied every inch of space in our quarters.

Our relegation to the ghetto illustrated that the Germans were able to segregate and control our population with absolute efficiency. We were virtually packed into the ghetto in the span of a workday. This ghetto was not enclosed in barbed wire. We were not hermetically sealed within walls. But we had no legal means to communicate with friends outside the ghetto. The ghetto meant we were not part of Polish society or the economy anymore, either. No one had any source of income. And we could not sneak out of the ghetto unless we were willing to risk our lives. I knew what had already happened in Vilna.

It made me question: was this just a holding pen for our relocation, or does all this mean we are about to be killed?

Those questions were answered later that day. Late in the afternoon, the ghetto teemed with German soldiers and Polish police. They were rounding up the Jewish men. They needed workers to pave a road, the soldiers said. The Gestapo escorted 21 men from the ghetto. My uncles, Zalman and Yoshe, were part of the group. Also with them was our *shtetl's* rabbi, Avraham Shmuel Kosczevky. Carrying nothing, everyone was herded into the forest.

Our house was elevated enough to allow us to see beyond the edge of the village and into the forest. From this vantage point, my mother and two aunts watched all 21 men march into the woods, just beyond the ghetto, where they were abruptly stopped. My Mom and aunts were whispering to one another when suddenly, their faces turned white. I could see their fear.

"Let me see!" I pleaded.

They stood there, holding one another, crying, screaming, and pulling their hair out.

I kept tugging on my mother's skirt. This time I insisted: "I want to see! I want to see! I want to see!" Reflexively, without realizing what she was doing, Mom picked me up. Then I remember being held by my mother with Aunt Henya and Aunt Basia standing next to us, scared, pale, with forlorn faces. We peered out the window and stood in silence. Our gazes fixed on the forest.

Suspended in my mother's arms, I watched total horror as the guards turned their venom on the men. A pack of howling *SS* dogs pulled on the people, viciously tearing into them. One dog had jumped on top of Rabbi Kosczevky and gnawed at his throat. I could hear the cries and screams from a distance. I shut my eyes and waited a few seconds. I was hoping that this was an illusion. Many were killed, bludgeoned at the hands of the Polish thugs, or bitten to death by the Nazi canines.

As I opened my eyes and looked to the edge of the village once more, the German soldiers were forcing the survivors to load up the bodies on wheelbarrows and take them into the forest, where they stopped near a bridge in an area called "the Bor." The few that survived were given shovels and told to dig a mass grave. When they finished, the German soldiers unloaded their weapons on the survivors. What I was watching was pure evil. Seeing our friends, neighbors, and loved ones holding onto one another as the Nazi soldiers fired their weapons was a level of unprincipled wickedness that I couldn't even imagine. I felt like it was a terrible nightmare. Many times I would say to myself: "O Lord, please help those people. Please help my family. Why are we trapped in this situation? Are we going to die?"

Every single person was shot. Age or status made no difference. The only thing that mattered was that the victims were Jewish. After the shooting, the victims were tossed into the ditch that they had been forced to dig.

As I looked, afraid and confused, I saw bodies moving in the trench. Some were still alive! Those poor people were ailing in pain, climbing on top of one another in desperation to get away. Some of the Germans fired their guns into the mass of bodies after they noticed the movement. Others used their bayonets to stab the bodies that had the appearance of life. This terror struck me hard. The soldiers had slaughtered every Jewish person in their sight. Those who were killed were friends of my parents. Probably all of them were customers of my Pop's. A lifetime ago, it seemed, we had celebrated Shabbat with them.

All of us in our ghetto dwelling were petrified. Were my uncles victims of the carnage? The adult women in my life were frozen in fear. It made me think of my father. "Where was Pop?" We haven't heard from him for many days. Was he among those that were killed?

CHAPTER 6

THAT EVENING IT started to rain.

My heart was still pounding from what had taken place in the forest. No one really made an attempt to calm the nerves of any of the children. I could see by their body language that Mom, Henya, and Basia were mourning over the fact that their husbands—which likely included my father—might have been killed in the pogrom.

We did not have a radio. We had no way of learning about what was happening in the world beyond our ghetto. Were the Germans behaving this way because the Soviets were beating them back? Had something happened to the partisans? Why are all these things happening to us? I was so terrified that I could not feel my body anymore. No one had any answers for what we could do to save ourselves.

Then the front door creaked open. A male figure appeared in the twilight. Pop! My complexion lit bright orange. Pop was alive! We all rushed to hug him.

He confirmed to us that my uncles, Zalman and Yoshe, had been killed in the forest. He asked, "Where are Henya and Basia?" We didn't know. There was no time to look for them. "We have to go before we are killed!" he said. Everything happened so quickly. "We have to go!" We then snuck out of our ghetto dwelling without anyone noticing. Unfortunately, we left without my aunts.

He insisted that we first sneak back to our house across the village to grab items we would need to survive. "We need more clothes for the children," he claimed. He also wanted to grab as much money as possible. He had some hidden away on the property. Pop's plan called for us to stay with his Christian friends outside Myadel, and he would likely need cash to pay them off.

For as visibly shaken as we were, my father was strong and stoic. In obedience, we grabbed the few things we had in our ghetto dwelling and then ran quietly to our home.

Chaim and I stood in the living room watching Nochum as our parents used sacks to pack up our winter clothing. Pop claimed there was no telling if we would ever return, but he insisted that we not bring anything else with us other than clothes. No toys. Not even an extra pair of shoes. None of us complained. Our parents were our security blankets.

We were in our house only minutes when the Germans and Polish guards discovered us. Two *SS* guards, seemingly intoxicated after their afternoon of killing Jews, stormed through the front door. "*Raus! Raus!*" they yelled. "Get out! Get out!" Ostensibly, the Polish police colluding with the Nazi soldiers informed the *SS* that we were back in our house.

"*Raus! Raus!*" They persisted. My father leaped in front of us children to protect us from the belligerent soldiers. There was a lot of yelling back and forth. None of us understood German, and I am sure they didn't speak Yiddish. The soldiers just pointed their rifles at my father while he stood there with his arms outstretched, begging for the Germans to let us go unharmed. "We will go back to the ghetto!" he pleaded. "Let us go!" "Let us go!" Pop was sweating profusely as he begged for mercy.

Suddenly, out of nowhere, one of the soldiers shot my father.

Pow!

In an apparent gunshot to his head, the bullet spun him a hundred and eighty degrees. *Thud!* He fell to the ground.

All of us except Nochum, who was horribly crying, stood there stunned, even emotionless as a guard kicked my father's arm to see if he was still alive. We knew in that sudden instant that we could not express emotion, or we might be shot as well. Within moments, blood seeped across the floor.

I wanted to cry. I wanted to scream. I wanted to hug him. Mom just held the three of us tightly while we all restrained our sobs. Then there was more shouting by the soldier who shot my father: "*Raus! Raus!*"

A Nazi soldier shoved us out the door while my father's body remained still and unattended to on the floor of our home. "*Raus! Raus!*" We were led back to our dwelling in the ghetto. The Germans hollered and pointed their guns at us the whole time. To this day, I cannot explain how my mother composed herself in front of us children. With Nochum in her arms, she shielded Chaim and me from the line of sight of the soldiers' weapons, which were now aimed at her back. As we got closer to the ghetto, the image of what had just happened became more unreal. I had a sinking feeling in the pit of my stomach. I finally began sobbing. Holding my mother's hand, I shut my eyes for a moment. I accepted the likelihood that we were all going to die.

When we arrived, one of the soldiers shoved us into our dwelling and barked something to us in German. We were wet and covered in mud. Inside of the house, we were surrounded by a multitude of people, including Aunt Basia, Aunt Henya, and Lile. Mom stood there unresponsive as her two sisters-in-law begged to know what happened. But it wasn't just my mother. The entire situation in the ghetto was somber. Many were still coming to terms with what happened earlier that day in the forest. No one had any idea about what just happened to my family. A lot of people were in shock.

I slid onto the floor and tried to catch my breath. I didn't know anything else I could do to help Mom or anyone else. So I bawled like a baby.

CHAPTER 7

I REMEMBER THE rain coming down the evening that my father was shot. It was a dark, cold, and damp evening. Looking out of the second-story window that night to where dozens of people were massacred, I recall, it was a gloomy and disconsolate day for many reasons. There were sounds of raindrops on the windowsill of our dwelling. With every alternating drop came an image of the past filled with sunshine and laughter, then darkness and sadness.

> *Our God and God of our ancestors.*
> *Remember Abraham, who flowed to You like water?*
> *You blessed him like a tree planted by streams of water.*
> *You rescued him from fire and water.*
> *He passed your test by planting good deeds by every source of water.*
> *For Abraham's sake, do not keep back water.*

We had been back in the ghetto only a short time, not even an hour when a figure appeared to us in the doorway.

"Hendel!" Mother cried out.

Was this a figment of my imagination? Could it be true? There he was. My father suddenly turned up. My Pop! He stood at a distance and beckoned Mom, Chaim, and me to hug him, which we did with great joy.

Wet, disheveled, with darkened bloodstains on his clothes, my father explained that he had been shot in the ear. He remained there on the floor, which fooled the soldiers into thinking he was dead. He had instantaneously decided it would be safer for us if he didn't resist. He sensed the *SS* men would not shoot him again if he lay there still and lifeless. He didn't mince words.

"We are leaving! Now!" Pop said. No one asked any questions. In great haste, with only the clothes on our backs and my father's Bible, we escaped into the forest. Thus began our flight to what would become the beginning of our displacement.

I started the journey on foot, running alongside my father. Mom held Nochum. Chaim was also traveling on foot. As we neared the forest, my father spotted a group of German soldiers and Polish police patrolling the streets. "Quiet," he cautioned. At that moment, one of the Polish police officers on horseback spotted us from a distance. His eyes met those of my father's. As he charged toward us, my father yelled out, "Stop! I have a gun." That wasn't true. He barrenly warned, "I will shoot you before you shoot me!"

"Wait! I am your friend," the soldier replied.

Pop responded, "How can you be my friend?"

"My mother-in-law had a dream last night that you were running and that I was going to save you," the mysterious soldier said.

This made no sense to me. Pop raised his eyebrows. "I'm warning you. Stop!"

He did. The soldier then took a deep breath and said slowly, "You come to my house, and I will save you."

In a moment of humanity, this police officer did more than just spare our lives. In that instant, this Polish national who served the wishes of an occupying force that represented the worst vestiges of humanity and had viciously governed over us with their guns, bayonets, whips, and dogs, showed compassion. But why now, I wondered?

After every atrocity he had been complicit in, he now wanted to help us. I understood when we arrived at his home. His mother-in-law was one of Pop's customers. She was in tears when we arrived. We were fed a meal and given information about the Germans.

We learned that the Germans had made a circle around the forest. They were slaughtering people as they ran for the woods. Pop pondered once again about taking up refuge in the forest, but the soldier advised that we would likely get caught if were made an escape attempt that night. He did suggest, however, that eventually, we should find our way into the forest. The Germans, he said, would never search deep into the forest because the partisans were so strong there.

While my brothers and I slept, Pop, Mom, and the soldier spent the night planning an eventual escape into the forest. From his days running the fabric store, Pop had saved enough money and acquired many friendships that a reasonable number of people indebted to him helped look after us.

Wary about the rummaging *SS* men, Pop made arrangements for us to hide at the farms of his friends as we gradually moved farther away from Myadel. We were fed. While we children slept, I'm sure my parents stayed up, ever vigilant of informants and the occupation police. We never stayed longer than a night or two before we moved to the next refuge.

Pop first took us to the home of a Christian that owned a farm not too far from the ghetto. I regretfully do not remember the name of this farmer. He was nevertheless an angel. He gave my father herbs to treat the bullet wound. Pop was also given a cow, which we used for food. We all realized that if the Germans discovered us in his house, they would kill him as well as us. We hid in his barn, underneath the hay, for no more than a week.

My father spent those days looking for a place for us to stay long-term. He had heard from friends that the Germans had eased up their surveillance at the edge of the village. Many people, Pop learned, had successfully escaped into the forest. He went there alone to investigate.

There he found clusters of people without food or comfortable places to live. People were just wandering around. He felt there was no way we could survive as a family in that environment.

On his way back to us, a Polish officer known in Myadel as the "Killer of the Jewish People" recognized him.

"Where are you going!" shouted the officer.

My father told him the truth. "I am running away."

"Go ahead," the officer replied. "You were good with my parents. You go ahead. I am not going to stop you."

He was lucky.

CHAPTER 8

ALEXANDER KURKEL WAS the man who saved my family. A Christian and a longtime customer of my father's fabric store before the Nazi occupation, Alexander hid us in his root cellar for many months. My father and Alexander were longtime friends since before I was born. Alexander's barn rested about 10 kilometers from Myadel. My Dad would often sleep there a night or two when he was traveling back and forth from Vilna on business. I cannot express how well the two got along. Despite Alexander's protest, my Dad paid him in gold pieces for our safekeeping. "You have to live. You have to survive," he would say to our father as he declined the recompense. The money was never important to Alexander, who understood that he wouldn't be able to spend it until after the war. Simply having extra pieces of gold would have drawn attention to Alexander's dissension against the Nazi occupiers.

For all intents and purposes, Alexander and his family deserve most of the credit for saving my family. He ended up placing us in the tiny root cellar of his barn. Alexander supplied us with several sheets of plywood the size of a Ping-Pong table on two carpenter's sawhorses. He gave us blankets to lie on. The cellar was slightly wider than the layers of plywood. And it had a window that my parents could see out of. There were times Alexander shared his food with us. It was difficult for him to set aside a daily meal without drawing too much attention that Jews were hiding in his cellar.

At night it was safest for my father to leave the cellar and rendez-vous with Alexander. Every so often, he would provide us with rolls of bread, potatoes, and milk. There were also times that Pop would leave at sunset to beg for food. Every time my father left, he was risking his life, our lives, and the lives of Alexander's family. He only went to people he knew, mostly former customers from his fabric store. Sometimes he came back with something to eat, but there were many nights he returned empty-handed. These journeys afforded him the opportunity to hear stories about the war, which kept us informed as to the *Wehrmacht's* movements. We were always excited about the prospect of the war ending when Pop returned with stories that the Germans were driven back by the Russians. We lived in this manner for ten months in that cellar.

As fate would have it, during one of my father's excursions beseeching food in and around Myadel, a friend told him that his sister, Henya, and her daughter, Lile, were in the Ponar Forest. Pop retorted, "Please, take me to them!" And the friend did. They found the two of them sitting next to a tree, looking like they had given up on life. Henya told him that they were part of a convoy of people that tried to escape to the Soviet Union. Aunt Basia was also part of the group. The tired group, including their children, knew that an escape plan carried with it peculiar dangers, but like my family, it was worth the risk rather than staying in the ghetto only to end up killed at the hands of a German soldier. They had paid a man to guide them out of Poland without being discovered by the SS. Their guide, unfortunately, was a swindler who cheated them out of their money. After leading them a few miles outside of Myadel, he took the money and left dozens of people stranded in the woods. When the group realized they were conned, some of the adults chose to tie their children to the trunks of trees as they continued on their trek to Russia. They hoped that some sympathetic people would find and rescue their children. They felt if both parents and children stayed back, both would be killed. Henya, however, refused to leave her daughter. She was too tired to walk and carry her daughter so they parted ways with Aunt Basia and sat there after having come to the realization that they would likely die in that forest. Henya and Lile decided that if they were going to die, they chose to do it together. But then by chance my father discovered them as he hiked through the forest. It was a miracle, we all believed.

Alexander allowed Henya and Lile to hide with us in the cellar. There were now seven of us to divide a daily loaf of bread and anything else Pop could obtain on his food excursions. Moreover, the additional people staying in our hideaway brought newfound attention to the activities at Alexander's house.

Before long, the word about our living in Alexander's cellar spread through the rumor mill to the wrong people. Sometime in the fall of 1943, his sister confronted him. "I heard you are keeping Jews," she said.

"How could you say such a thing?" he responded. "Of course, I'm not." The response convinced her to leave at the moment. Twenty-four hours later, however, she returned and reproached him with indignation.

"Alexander, you lied to me," she alleged. "I know you're keeping Jews. Tomorrow I am going to bring the *SS* to check your house."

Alexander didn't have to say anything to us. We knew it was time to go.

We slipped away, undetected, miles into the forest. We later learned the *SS* arrived the next day.

Alexander was with us when we fled. He brought his horse. Chaim Zelman, Nochum, and I were allowed to rest upon it as Alexander led us deep into the woods. A gloom crept over me the same way vines gradually make way up the side of a building. I didn't feel safe. "How far are we going?" I finally asked anyone who would hear me. "Where are we going to stay?" I was terrified.

Mom said, "We are going to make a home here."

"In the forest?" I responded.

She said nothing.

"Mom?"

She remained silent.

"Mom?"

She looked ahead, into the mystifying wilderness.

"Mom!"

Mom and Pop glanced at one another with recalcitrant fear. Then she grudgingly replied, "Things will work out all right." I accepted the answer with, of course, little enthusiasm.

Before the sunset, we had traveled what felt like an eternity through the dense woodland of the Ponar Forest before stopping at a large Banyan tree that grew along a bank. "Where are we?" "Do we know how to get home?" "What do we do now?" My eyes were heavy, and I wanted so badly to rest. I looked at my Pop and Mom. I could tell they too wanted to sleep. There was a ghost of a smile on Mom's face, though she looked as if she knew we had more to do before lying down to sleep.

My father and Alexander dug out a *Zimlanka*, or cave, next to the large tree. Around us, the forest breathed. Gusts of wind had a cooling sensation. Butterflies fluttered through the breeze. Squirrels danced overtop as they hopped from one tree branch to the next. I watched the sun fall steadily beyond the horizon, and the moon made its way across the arch of the heavens. It got colder as we waited for Pop and Alexander to finish excavating our new home. Through the early evening and into the dark night, they dug a cave wide and deep enough into the embankment to fit the seven of us. We possibly had enough room to fit a few more people if we must. No matter if there were seven or ten people hiding out in that dugout, there wasn't any headspace for anyone to stand. And there certainly was no privacy.

To keep the cavern from collapsing, Pop and Alexander brought with them wooden planks to use for the ceiling and walls. The residual dirt from the cave's interior was shoveled into potato sacks, which were thrown onto the back of Alexander's horse and taken to a nearby stream. Alexander emptied the brush into the water in an attempt to not give the Germans or their collaborators any indication that anyone was hiding in the area. We used pine tree branches and other shrubbery to conceal the entrance into our *Zimlanka*.

That dugout was our home for a few months. Mom and Pop agreed it was too dangerous for us to stay in that spot. While they trusted Alexander with our lives, it was just too risky for us to remain in the original *Zimlanka* permanently. What if Alexander was interrogated? Everyone has a breaking point. So Pop spent days digging out a new *Zimlanka* on the other side of the stream. This spot became our home for the next eighteen months, through many seasons, climates, illnesses, and while under the shadow of patrolling *SS* men and their Polish collaborators.

Of course, at the time, we had no idea how long we would be displaced in a manmade cavern. We held out hope that the Germans would be driven out of Poland by the Soviets in a few weeks' time. That was wishful thinking. We mentally prepared ourselves to spend the rest of our lives in that *Zimlanka*. Situated as an omnipresent woodland along the border of Myadel, this endless forest had suddenly become our sanctuary for an indeterminate amount of time. Its swamps and streams and its vegetation and wildlife were now part of my new home. Of course, we knew that we were not the first to take shelter in the Ponar Forest. Partisans had been calling it home for the past year. At that moment, however, we were all praying to God to protect us. We also thanked Him for our father's dear friend, Alexander. We took solace in the fact that we were still together.

CHAPTER 9

IT WAS ALREADY winter when we settled into our *Zimlanka*. We were in no way prepared to handle Eastern Europe's bone-chilling climate. In addition to helping my Pop dig out the cave, Alexander supplied us with a few blankets. We laid some out on top of the dirt and straw that we made into our floor. Several additional blankets were used to keep us warm. We nestled into our home inside the earth, lying shoulder to shoulder, for days on end.

Just as we settled into our dugout, Pop set out to discover what happened to our mother's family in Vilna. Of course, he had a hunch they hadn't survived the Nazi *aktions* of a few weeks earlier. Still, my mother insisted that they try. Pop was able to make contact with a person who was in touch with the partisans fighting outside of Vilna. He returned with the terrible news that we were too late. My mother's family—her parents and siblings and several cousins—had been taken to the Ponary Forest and killed alongside 75,000 Jews. Obviously, the news affected all of us. It hit my mother particularly hard, but she remained steadfast in front of us.

Time stood still. Sunlight was shining for fewer hours each day. Temperatures seemingly dropped colder with each passing sun. And colder. Much colder than I ever remembered. I could only think – I want the jacket that I left in Myadel. And my bed. I want to run around in my back yard. I want to play in my Pop's orchard field. Oh, to be sitting in the back corner of his fabric store as delightful customers walked in and out, speaking with my father about trivial things. Now, we are consumed with concern about getting discovered. Ever vigilant. Always quiet. And yet, time moved so slowly.

Leaving tracks in the snow for someone to find us was of great concern to us all. It was decided that my father would be the only one to leave the *Zimlanka* without permission. Almost every night, Pop disappeared to the surrounding villages in search of food. The six of us stayed safe in the cave, holding our breath until he returned. He was always so assiduous in his effort to cover his footprints. Some times he returned empty-handed. Occasionally he arrived with a loaf of bread, milk, and usually potato *babkas* that we rationed for days. The *babkas* became my favorite meal. It is a dish made of shredded potatoes, onions, and eggs fried in oil. When it was in season, Pop would pick us blueberries and mushrooms.

I was always worried about my father. He was doing so much to keep us alive. Every time he went hunting for food, Pop would reassure that he would return. I can still picture how calming he was. Some nights he would say, "Honey, I will return in the morning with breakfast." Other evenings he comforted, "Lile, Nothing will harm me. I am a pal with everyone I seek out for food." Every time his voice hit me like a physical jolt that this could be the last time I ever see him. Each night, I still envision the moment of him getting shot in the ear. It scares me.

After we were in hiding in the cave for about three months, Pop returned from one of his all-night food-collecting expeditions and told us we were going to Alexander's for an evening. I was so stunned by the news. In my mind, I asked the question, "Why don't we do this every night?" I was simply too young to understand the risk.

At Alexander's house that night, we behaved like royalty. Our hosts covered the windows with dark blinds. There was joke-telling. And laughing. There was talk of the war. And we listened to music on the radio. My parents didn't want us, children, to worry about getting caught. They let us enjoy a very palatable homemade potato soup at Alexander's dinner table. I then shared a bed with Alexander's daughter. It was a fleeting yet special night.

Then as expected, we were back in our dugout within twenty-four hours, where our routine was pretty standard. In the morning, Pop usually slept in since he spent most evenings wandering the countryside in search of food. During those morning hours, Mom gave us lessons in history and mathematics. And she spoke to us about poetry, which was one of her passions from the time she studied at the university in Vilna. We just lied there listening and re-listening to her lessons. She didn't have any props. She spoke extemporaneously, recalling everything from memory. Neither did we have notebooks or pencils. And obviously, we didn't have desks. We had to remember everything. Asking questions was an expectation.

In the evening, Pop would teach us scriptures from the *Tanakh*, or Hebrew Bible. He knew every story. He often sat with his back to the shrubbery that we used to block the entrance of our *Zimlanka*. Enough sunlight and moonlight shone into our cave, which enabled him to read passages from the Scripture. Though he knew every story in the Bible by heart, he would read to us certain passages and then elaborate on all the stories. There were times he handed us the Bible and told us to read. Rightfully so, he would often repeat a passage from Jeremiah 31:2 that says, "So says the Lord, In the wilderness, the people who had escaped the sword found favor." After Pop gave his message, he would expect us to ask him questions. This is how we learned the history of Jewish people. It was our *chedar*.

This went on for weeks until I got really sick.

I had contracted pneumonia. My parents were gravely concerned that I wouldn't survive. One night during this awful winter, my father carried me in his arms many miles to a friend's house, where he left me. I do not recall the name of my father's friend. It certainly wasn't Alexander, but he allowed me to stay with him for two weeks. He ended up saving my life.

Wrapped in blankets, I was placed on top of a brick bread oven as I recovered. The oven wasn't that high off the ground. And the combination of its brick exterior and the blankets prevented me from burning up. I slept most of the time. For the short periods that I was awake, I was given food to eat. And I looked forward to every night because my father would walk through the forest to see if I was recovering. Luckily, German soldiers never wandered into this man's house. If they discovered I was there, everyone would have been killed. And I was concerned that I might panic and reveal where my family was staying.

My father aroused me at dusk one night when I was feeling better and carried me back to the *Zimlanka*. I don't know the month or the day, but I recall seeing stars for the first time in many days as my father held me in his arms. There was a seasonable chill in the dark night. It was a happy moment for everyone to see me healthy. We nestled into our dugout once again as a family. My mom held me tight in her arms that night.

CHAPTER 10

AS WINTER TURNED into spring and spring into the summer of 1943, we all held on to the hope that in another week, the Germans would be defeated. Often when Pop went out looking for food, he would return with reports that the Russians were pushing the Germans back. "The Germans aren't doing so good," he would say. Once, he told us about an uprising at the ghetto in Warsaw. Occasionally he returned with stories of Soviet victories over the Germans as well as American victories over the Italians. But then another week would pass, and we were still in the same predicament. We never grew comfortable in our situation.

We had been in hiding in the earth for almost a full year. The situation along the Eastern Front seemed unchanged. My father returned once with horrific news. I overheard him say to Mom that no one was left in the Myadel ghetto. Everyone had been taken in cattle cars to the concentration camps where he assumed they were killed.

By the summer of 1943, Polish nationals, German *SS* men, and refugees hiding in the forest inhabited the area around Myadel. Most escapees, however, were not like us. They had escaped into the forest and found protection with the partisans. Under my father's authority, we did not go with the Jewish partisans. In fact, we did everything in our power to avoid being discovered by not only the Nazis but also the partisans. The Myadel partisans, aging anywhere from teenagers to middle-aged men, and numbering in the dozens, waged a ghastly guerilla war against the Nazis. They became notorious for blowing up train tracks, cutting telephone wires, ambushing German convoys, and other acts of subversion.

Pop understood the dangers of getting involved with the partisans since we were a family with three small children. As it turned out, he was right. Many of the families with young children were left behind, as they could not keep up with the partisans' movements. Moreover, during rare occasions that the Germans entered into the forest in search of Jews, many of the children were left behind. We heard horrifying stories about parents that tied their children to tree trunks in hopes that someone might find and rescue them. They were often discovered and killed by Nazi soldiers.

Pop's reason for hiding from the partisans was also so we could stay together as a family. We heard rumors about cases when partisans encountered men my father's age. The expectation was that all men would join the resistance. Any time a man refused to take up arms, the partisans considered him a Nazi collaborator and would kill him. Pop was worried that he would be forced into the resistance, which would leave us on our own. We wouldn't learn this until later, but a group of partisans led by Bernard Druskin lived north of us in the Ponar Forest near Vilna. The Russians seemingly delivered dynamite, arms, and ammunition for Druskin's soldiers by flying overtop the forest and dropping crates of supplies by way of a parachute. After the partisans were supplied with arms, they would steal the identities of Polish nationals so they could pass as non-Jews in town. From those positions on the inside, they would ambush German soldiers.

In the Perelaz Forest, southwest of our *Zimlanka*, was the band of Jewish partisan fighters led by the four fugitives from the Nowogrodek ghetto. The four fugitives were known as the Bielski brothers, who had hundreds of followers consisting of men, women, and children. While some of their followers eventually took up arms, rumors spread all the way to the Narach region that they mistreated and sometimes killed those who refused to fight. While my father never directly heard about the Bielski brothers, stories about actions they were involved in had reached Myadel. This is what frightened my father. He was always so worried about being taken away or killed by partisans. His main concern throughout this nightmare we were living was the safety of our family. He refused to be separated from us. "We have to stay together," he always said.

We had been hiding in the cave my father dug with Alexander for almost a year already when Pop learned that too many people in Myadel had discovered the area where we were hiding. He had already dug us a new *Zimlanka* in an area of the forest located in the opposite direction where we had spent the previous 12 months. We stood for a moment as we watched Pop do his best to hide our cave. Then my parents moved us swiftly from one cave to the other.

The weather was changing. Days were getting warmer. Nights were still chilly. Vegetation and foliage were born-again and plentiful. Yet, we were always hungry, and we had grown very skinny. Despite our shrinking bodies, Chaim, Nochum, Lile, and I rarely complained about the food. At our young ages, we understood the importance of holding onto hope that the war's end was right around the corner.

I remember defecation being a sensitive and awkward daily affair. Our latrine was a solitary bucket that we shared during the day. It was difficult to bear the stench as it sat in the corner of the cave. Occasionally, my father risked emptying the bucket during the day-time. It was routine, however, that at dusk, he would dump it in the stream.

Once I noticed my mother cleaning blood from her inner thighs. I asked her, "What is that?" as her legs were smeared in blood. She dismissed my query. "It's nothing, Lile," she averred. Of course, she was menstruating, but at the time, this was something I was unfamiliar with. I don't remember this happening to her more than once. She may have lost the ability to menstruate, or she figured out a way to hide her monthly period from us during the time we were in hiding. My mother had no pads. Nor did she have any privacy to arrest the flow of blood.

I'm sure my seeing her in that condition mortified her. Many questions ran through my preadolescent mind during that one episode. Is she going to be okay? Is this something serious? How will she get treated for an injury that caused that amount of blood? I watched as she used a dust rag to clean herself in full view of us children.

It didn't take long until lice besieged our dugout. Those little bugs were everywhere. They feasted on all of us. The lice were in our hair. They were found in our clothing. We slept on blankets that were beleaguered with lice.

Every day we took time to de-louse our hair and clothing. We combed each other's hair. We shook out our clothing. No sooner did we put our clothes back on that we were scratching and clawing at creeping lice all over our bodies. For me, this was the worst part of my experience in the cave. It was worse than the feeling of starvation. I never grew used to the infestation of those tiny parasites crawling through my hair and all over my body. I think I lost more sleep going mad about the lice than I did worrying about the Germans finding us.

One might think that these conditions put immense strain on our family, especially with four young children sharing a small space with nothing to do to pass the time. I say with confidence, however, that it didn't damage us. Of course, nothing about living in that cave was pleasant. My parents' hopefulness in those dire circumstances taught me an important lesson: there is always one thing that I can control no matter how bad things are. I will always have the freedom to choose how I react to a situation. That was something the Germans couldn't take away from me. It was something that living in a cave couldn't take from me. And at that moment, I chose to persevere.

CHAPTER 11

WE NEVER KNEW what day of the week it was. And it was difficult keeping track of the changing seasons. Like many Mid-Atlantic winters and springs, unpredictable and ever-changing weather patterns would bring warm days when it was supposed to be a wintery season and cold days when it was supposed to be warm. None of us kept track of the passing days. If asked, I cannot confidently say the exact number of days we hid in that dank and wretched cave.

I remember one morning when I woke up with an unexplained sense of optimism and belief that something good was about to happen. It was a chilly and cloudless morning; the sun pierced the shrubbery of our *Zimlanka*. It must have been springtime in 1944. I shared with my mother the inexplicable dream I had over the night.

I said, "Mom! We're going to be free!"

"Yeah, yeah," she said. "Why do you say that?"

Then I told her about my premonition. The five of us looked healthy and were dressed in clean clothes. We were in the family orchard back in Myadel. None of us was doing anything special. We were carefree and just walked along as if the war was a distant memory. The peacefulness of the impression that my family was living free on a warm and beautiful day resonated most with me when I woke up.

"Mom, I don't know when we'll be free, but I know it's going to be when it's a warm day," I proclaimed.

"It is, huh?" She replied. "Well, Lile, you are the one with all the *mazel*." Mom called me the family's good luck charm. She embraced me. When I looked up, her smile had widened. "You have been ever since you were born in the sac." That singular line, "born in the sac," was her classic riposte. It was her way of telling me I was special. And perhaps in this time of peril, my dream could bring hope and courage to all of us stuck in that cave.

CHAPTER 12

IF FORCED TO choose a time that I favored living in the forest, the summer months would be it. While warm outside, our *Zimlanka* remained cool. Though tempted to break out of the cave and frolic through the forest, the dueling hot and cold temperature was a nice contrast to the erratic wintery weather we already endured. During the summer months, Pop cut back on the number of times he ran off in search of food. Instead, he cavorted around the woods, looking for edible vegetation. He mainly found berries and mushrooms for us to eat.

Early after the weather broke, my father led us all to Alexander's house. It was one of our few surreptitious journeys through the woods to get a good meal and to wash our clothes as well as our bodies. This journey, I remember particularly well because my trip on foot was laden with pain. I only had one pair of shoes. After many months in hiding, my feet had grown too big. It was hardly an issue when hiding in the *Zimlanka* because my parents prohibited me from leaving. So I hardly put them on. On this journey, however, I had to wear them. The trek was long, and neither my mother nor my father had the strength to carry me the distance to Alexander's house.

Trips to Alexander's were always dangerous. This time, Pop felt the risk of encountering the Nazis did not exceed the need to get us cleaned up and fed. "The Germans are scared to enter the woods because of the partisans," he told us before we set out for Alexander's farm. "We shouldn't encounter the Germans until we get to town."

Whether reassured by my father's words or simply numb to terror after many months of hiding, I felt no fear as we crept through the woods. My feet hurt, though. "Keep up!" Pop commanded as my emaciated body weaved to avoid exposed roots and tree branches that hung as low as my eye line. I didn't remember the trip being this long before. He pulled me by the hand as he led the way. Mom was in the back, making sure none of us fell behind. Henya and Lile were with us, too. No one said a word except Pop. "Be still!" "Crouch down!" "Keep up!" "We're almost there!" he instructed. We obeyed.

In the pitch-black, we reached Alexander's house. With a subtle knock on the door, our gracious host welcomed us with a small meal, a bath, and clean clothes.

My parents allowed me to listen to their conversation about the war. I sat silently for a long time listening to what Alexander had to say. The Russians are near.

"It's only a matter of time."

"Wonderful, Alexander! How close are they?"

"The last word on the radio was that the Germans were driven out of Polotsk."

There is more, he said. "There are camps." I noticed the pain in his eyes. My father didn't flinch. He knew. My mother knew. I guess they wanted me to know. "Mommies. Daddies. Kids. No one survives these camps." He suggested that I was one of the fortunate ones; that my brothers, and Lile, and I were lucky to have my parents and Aunt Henya, who took risks to keep us all safe. He was right. But even then, I found it hard to accept living in a world where people were killed because of religion, or health, or social status. Even at my young age, I accepted the fact that some unfortunate children would die while in the arms of their mother. I first learned this wartime reality before we escaped to the forest when that one SS guard shot my father right in front of us. How could someone do that? How could a human being shoot a man with his wife and three little children standing right there?

I believed in all my heart that my parents were wonderful. I knew that my brothers and I were lucky to be alive. But I struggled to accept my own survival in such an ungodly place.

I was robbed of my childhood long ago. It had been many months now since my freedom and youth had been stolen from me by men with guns. Now, as the war seemed to be nearing its end, I thought, how am I supposed to recover after witnessing such savagery?

Linda Schwab

Linda's maternal grandmother, Tzire
Dimentsyein Aronovitch, 1920

Linda's maternal grandfather, Rabbi
Anshel Aronovitch, 1920

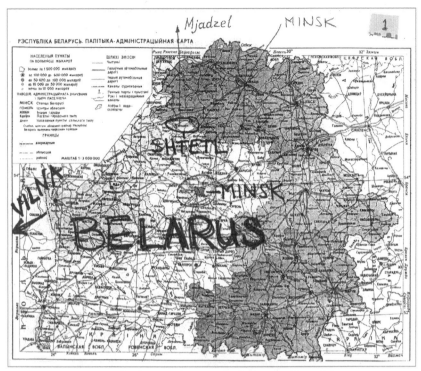

Map of Belarus indicating the location of Myadel.

Alexander Kurkel in his home many years after World War II.
Linda credits him for saving her family.

Linda and her family at the Fohrenwald
Displaced Persons Camp in 1948.

A soccer match inside the Fohrenwald DP camp, ca. 1949.

One of Linda's classes inside the DP camp, ca. 1948.

Linda with her Displaced Persons classmates on a field trip to the
Rhine River in 1947.

This Hamlu, or gold medal, was awarded to Linda for her victory in the Fohrenwald sports festival. At age 13, Linda was the camp's decathlon champion.

Linda's mother and father inside the Fohrenwald DP Camp, 1947.

The first photograph taken of Linda's family
in the United States, 1949.

Linda on the steps of the Pennsylvania Capitol Building receiving a
writing award in 1953.

Linda's mother and father in 1960.

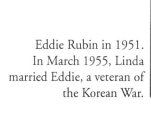

Eddie Rubin in 1951.
In March 1955, Linda
married Eddie, a veteran of
the Korean War.

Linda and Eddie at the bar mitzvah held in honor of their son Stephen in 1977.

Linda with Fay Snowiess (left) in 2005. Fay taught Linda to speak English when they were teenagers.

Linda with her second husband, Morris Schwab, in 2003.

Mother's Day in Harrisburg, Pa, May 2004.
Back row (left to right): Erica, Eddie, and Ellen.
Front Row: Ali, Caroline and Lauren.

Portrait of Linda in 1985.

The 80th birthday celebration for Linda (front row fifth from the left)
with family in Harrisburg, 2017.

CHAPTER 13

"LET'S GO!" my father roared. "Put your shoes on! It's time to go!"

It was a July morning in 1944. My Dad had just returned from the village. He was still catching his breath as he entered the *Zimlanka*. "I'm not kidding. We have to move!" He was told that the Germans were on their way into the forest with orders to destroy everything in sight. While this was a sign that the Russians had overtaken the *Wehrmacht*, it meant that we couldn't sit idly by as the Germans ravaged as much of the Polish countryside as possible.

As the Germans retreated, they intended to slow down the Soviet advance on their positions and to thwart attacks by the partisans by setting ablaze the forest and all the villages in their midst. Thousands of Nazi soldiers formed a *tsop*, or braid of soldiers positioned about 20 yards apart, and marched through the Ponar Forest, annihilating everything. Which meant, if we continued hiding out in the cave, we might be burned alive. "We won't survive if we stay here," my Dad cautioned. He had been right about everything for the last eighteen months. Why wouldn't we listen to him now?

Though he felt that we had a bit of time before the Germans would arrive at our location, Pop quickly packed a rucksack with blankets and our few possessions. He instructed us to put on our shoes and make haste out of the forest. We ran until we found a meadow that had been prepped for the coming harvest. He stopped abruptly. Following his lead, we stopped, too. It was fleeting, but for just a moment, we all looked out upon the open field; streaks of the shimmering sun shone beautifully on the green grass. I saw this all before in my dream. Is this the day we are liberated? I was overcome with hope. And then we returned to reality.

"We have to split up," Pop commanded. "If the Germans find us all in one place, that'll be the end of all of us." Two haystacks rested in the open field. My father ran to one of the stacks and motioned for Aunt Henya and Lile to come with him. He placed them inside the haystack. He then signaled to my mother to bring Nochum and follow him to the other. He tucked them inside the second haystack. He then looked around for a third, but couldn't find one for Chaim and me. Instead, he found a pile of brush across the field. Pop, Chaim, and I hurried to it. Dad dug a hole, and we used the blankets that we brought with us from the *Zimlanka* to lie on. We then pulled the brush over top of us to use as camouflage. We hid there for what seemed to be at least twenty-four hours.

We waited and waited for the moment that those dreaded Nazi boots would be heard in the distance. I had become so thirsty as we laid there that I beckoned my father for water. "Please, Pop," I remember saying. My father didn't have water in our rucksack, so he took his bony hand and pressed our only spoon deep into the mud. "Look at me, Lile." He said as he fixed on my eyes. I knew he saw weakness. "This will get you through the night." He handed me the spoon with only a few drops of water. "Consider this a special remedy," he said. I was able to wet my lips, and I shut my eyes in relief.

Pop's voice was tired, and yet he was determined to make sure we were doing all right. "We will survive — all of us. We will survive," he repeated. He conceived a plan to make frequent checkups on Mom's and Aunt Henya's haystacks. He was afraid, however, that he might not be able to find his way back to our hiding spot. The field was vast. It was getting darker. But it was important for everyone's sanity that he checkup on each and every one of us. In order to get to the haystacks and back without getting lost, Pop had to teach Chaim how to whistle. He ordered my brother to whistle every few seconds while he was in the field so that he could use the sound to find his way back to us.

This was Pop's routine all day and night. Every few hours, he made his rounds, ensuring everyone that we will make it out of this nightmare. Chaim's whistles would guide him back every time. I helped by keeping a lookout for Germans coming from the opposite direction.

In mid-morning, the Germans reached us. Pop grabbed my arm, put his fingers on my lips, and told me to be quiet. "Do you hear that?" he whispered. The Germans were marching in a *tzep*, or phalanx, and were headed directly for us. With fixed bayonets, the soldiers trudged through the forest in fixed positions about 10-15 yards apart; they high-stepped branches and bushes as they moved closer and closer to our hiding spot. "We don't want them to know we are here," he said. A stocky officer with a resolute gaze yelled orders as he waved his gun around. We were all petrified they would stumble upon our trench and kill us. After almost two years in hiding, our lives arrived at this final moment. Chaim and I lay there, huddled in the arms of our father.

I was petrified. My limbs were frozen. "Daddy," I breathed.

"Shh!" He begged. He squeezed us tighter as a lump formed in my throat. Hard. I know that we matter more to him than his own safety, and if being silent and still with dozens of Nazi soldiers closing in on our hiding place means we will be safe, I believed him.

"Ein anderer Morgen, ein anderer Wald." "Another morning, another forest," I heard a soldier say as the phalanx of troops walked within earshot of where we were hiding the brush.

Pop fixed his gaze on the soldiers. The sounds of the German boots came within several yards of us before the burly soldier barked an order: *"Ein shleesen recht!"* "Turn to the right!" Abruptly, by the grace of God, the entire platoon of soldiers moved away from our position. Instead of marching right into our hiding place, they missed us! It was God's will to allow us to live. I think of it as God parting the Red Sea for Moses. To this day, when I see German boots in a movie or a still photograph,

I always flashback to the moment when those boots came to a halt as the command *Ein shleesen recht* was given.

The Germans were now marching in the direction of Aunt Henya and Lile. So my father peered out of our hiding place without the Germans noticing. He needed to see that they were all right.

"It's okay. I am sure they are safe," he told us. We didn't hear any shooting, so we assumed that my aunt and cousin were also safe.

We laid there in deep silence. As I rested there, perverse images of soldiers, wounded people screaming, and wreckage moved fast through my mind. But so did thoughts of children laughing and playing. After about an hour, my father went to see if my mother, brother, aunt, and cousin were safe.

"We're safe," Aunt Henya said to Pop. "The Germans just left!"

Near the Aunt Henya and Lile haystack was an embankment. My father ran to the top to see where the Germans had gone. He stood there with his eyes beaming, looking intensely into the distance. He gestured that the German soldiers were not in sight. Large fires, however, were scattered across the meadow. He signaled us to come out of hiding. We rushed, climbing to the top of the mound. I stood close to Pop. He was holding back tears. Much of the countryside and our section of the forest where we had spent the last eighteen months had been set ablaze by the fleeing soldiers. He put his arms around all of us. "We are still together," he said. I felt a sense of ease. The momentary feeling of freedom overwhelmed all of us.

My Pop did it again. He saved us.

CHAPTER 14

WE STOOD IN silence for a short time. The warm air against my skin made me think of the dream I had earlier that spring. I felt a sense of comfort. We all did. I looked up at my parents. They both winked and gave me a big smile of satisfaction. Everything felt surreal.

My father instructed us to return to our *Zimlanka* and wait as he ran into town, see to if it was safe to come out of hiding.

"I will be back later," Pop said. "No matter what's going on in town, it is likely we will sleep here again tonight."

We nestled in and waited anxiously for his return. We were all a happy family. The wait that evening, however, was not easy. I clung tightly to Mom, thinking about my father every moment he was gone. Thankfully, Pop returned hours later with the news that all of the Germans had, in fact, retreated. He told us that the Soviets were moving into Myadel to secure the area.

"We are free!" he assured us. "But we need to wait a little longer before we go home." So we settled in for one final night in our dugout.

I awoke the next morning to the sound of planes flying overhead. They were Russian planes!

I found my parents outside the cave, looking up at the sky. They were discussing a plan for our return to Myadel. "Come here," Mom said. "Lile, please stay close to your brothers and your cousin as we think of what to do." She then pointed to a patch in the grass where she suggested we sit and wait. I sat next to Chaim and watched my parents and Aunt Henya consider our next move.

"Okay, everyone. Let's walk this way," Mom said.

We hiked through the same meadow where we had eluded the Germans 24 hours earlier. My father led us a couple of hours before we came upon a paved road. "That's where we are going," Pop said as he patted the top of my head and ran his fingers through my hair. Already positioned on the side of the road below us was a multitude of jubilant people. They stood there, cheering as tanks and jeeps rolled by. It was a bit confusing. White stars were painted onto the sides of each vehicle. The Red Army, we understood for earlier days under the occupation of the Soviets, used the red star. We later learned that the Red Army was using American equipment sent to aid the Russians on the Eastern Front. Apparently, the Russians didn't have the time to change the stars from white to red. It was in that moment, nevertheless, that the feeling of hunger and the level of fear that I typically felt had escaped me. The Russians had liberated us. We are truly free! I was never so happy to see Russians!

We rushed to get as close as possible to the tanks. We were in awe. The soldiers seemed friendly as they waved and yelled to us in Russian. Though none of us understood a word, we took pleasure in seeing our liberators. I remember resting beside my brothers as dozens of tanks and jeeps drove in the direction of Myadel. I enjoyed a great sense of comfort just lying there.

Suddenly, one of the Soviet tanks stopped. A soldier hopped down and approached Chaim, who sat there motionless. His mouth opened but said nothing. I stood next to him. Like my brother, my instinct told me not to move. So I didn't. To the soldier, I am sure all of us looked pale, emaciated, filthy, and wholly malnourished. We were walking skeletons. Our ungodly condition must have stunned the Russian as he took off his helmet and placed it on my brother's head. It was a gift for him to treasure.

My heart pounded loudly, but Pop made me relax. "Well, look at that," he shouted cheerfully. "It's not every day that you're given an army helmet from a Russian. Don't tell too many people. You'll be in their army tomorrow."

I laughed as Chaim passed the helmet around. We all took turns trying it on.

We were hungry. We were tired. We were exhausted.

We were joyful.

CHAPTER 15

IN AREAS LEFT behind by the fleeing Germans, the joyful celebrations were nonexistent. No cheers or festivities. There was only eerie silence as much of the countryside was burned down. Even our *shtetl* had lost its identity. "The Myadel that we once knew doesn't exist anymore," Mom would often say. Though the structure of the village's two synagogues could still be seen, the roofs and interior of each building were destroyed. There was still the odor of livestock rotting in burned barns and at the edge of the forest. The devastation was as bad to the west, where in addition to Poland's urban ruins, most of the farms were out of operation, and most of the railroad tracks were unusable. To the east in Byelorussia, we learned that the Germans had destroyed most of the countryside all the way to Minsk. In a sense, the Ponary Forest, stretching from the Russian border in the east to Warsaw in the west, had become the graveyard of our people. We would eventually learn that the Jewish death toll was estimated at more than 6 million persons. This was equivalent to more than 70 percent of the Jewish population in Europe. Everyone in my family instantly felt the impact of this Holocaust, as it eventually came to be known.

Meanwhile, the three properties my parents owned before the war were already occupied. The house we lived in on Jewish Street was turned into a bank. Our second house was made into a dairy farm. And the house my father built in our orchard became a state-owned farm. We ended up finding a small house to live in. The original owners were victims of Germany's genocide.

It was nearly August 1944 when the Soviets drove the Germans out of our region of Poland. The war dragged on for another nine months as the Red Army closed in on Berlin. Since the war's end was still unpredictable, my father was expected to register as a Polish soldier in the Red Army. On the morning of his registration, we walked as a family to the draft office. We were all crying. Inside the office, however, Pop's former boss from the chemical company spotted him. He pulled my father aside to meet with his supervisor—a Russian officer—and negotiated a non-combatant duty. Pop was reassigned to his pre-war job as the manager of the Reicheem Leshoseh sap company. His role as *Nachalnick*, or head of Reicheem Leshoseh, meant that he could employ his own platoon of sap collectors. To find workers, he returned to the forest, where he knew men were still hiding. They were afraid to come out because they, too, knew they would be forced into the Red Army. The only other option, they believed, was that they might be shipped to Siberia. "I am going to save you," my father told them. "I am going to give you a job, give you papers, and you are going to work for me in Myadel. Trust me." Single-handedly, my father saved up to 60 people who returned with him to work.

The Reicheem Leshoseh Company was able to sell syrup throughout Poland. He sometimes traveled as far away as Minsk. He and his men were able to keep most of the profits for themselves.

We tried to establish normal lives after the war. My older brother and I even started attending a school that reopened in Myadel. And yet we could never escape the vestiges of war. One day the Russians discovered two Polish nationals that helped the Nazis commit war crimes on the Jewish people in our village. The Russians troops held a show trial complete with a public execution in the center of the village. After a small excelsior brass band played a few numbers, the exhibition's signature event came when the prisoners were tied to nooses and handcuffed as they stood on the bed of a truck. Then, after a few speeches, the truck pulled away, leaving the two war criminals to hang. Their bodies were kept on display in the village square for several days.

The Russian troops seemed disorganized. The longer they were stationed in Myadel, the more menacing they became to my family. The Soviet soldiers, dressed in green military jackets, shoulder boards, and the red five-pointed star attached to the front of their military khaki visor caps, often harassed us for being the only remaining Jews in Myadel. Their anti-Semitic comments intensified the uncertainty and anxiety in our lives. Although he had a prominent job, I was terrified that my father would be taken away from us. He must have had the same feeling. Soon after the Germans surrendered in May 1945, it became apparent that Pop had no real expectation of independence under the supervision of the Soviets. During one of his trips to pick up a friend at the train station, my father was warned to leave Poland. My father's friend had retreated to the Soviet Union in September 1941 when the Germans had broken its wartime truce with the Soviets. He ended up in a Siberian labor camp. When the war ended, Stalin allowed those that wanted to go back to Poland to return.

"Hendel, don't stay in Poland," he advised. "You have children to raise. This land is like fire. The Russians will keep you as long as you're working. But as soon as they have no purpose for you, they will either kill you or send you to jail."

No one understood better than my father how to elude anti-Semitic virulence. So when Pop returned, he and Mom jointly decided that we would try to leave Europe. They spoke most about moving to Palestine (later-Israel). The way to Israel, however, was to find our way to American soldiers stationed in Germany. Through friends, my father learned that there was a Jewish refugee agency in Lodz, a city in the western part of Poland, about 600 kilometers west of Myadel and about 130 kilometers west of Warsaw, that was assisting Jews that were trying to get to the American zones of Germany.

My father refused to leave without my Aunt Basia, who had escaped with the Soviet army just before the German invasion years earlier and was living in Siberia last he knew. Pop left for Russia to find her. He traveled across all of Siberia and somehow discovered her. According to him, there was only a small amount of resistance to the rendition of his sister. He carried papers that both proved she lived in Myadel before the war and that he has resettled with our family in the *shtetl* now that the war was over. They released her!

Sometime during the summer of 1945, we packed up our belongings, including vodka, tobacco, and extra items we could use to barter. With Basia, we left our home for good. I never saw Myadel again.

We rode a horse and buggy north to the railroad station in Vilna, stopping first to say goodbye to Alexander and his family. In order to get a seat on a train, we needed a reservation months earlier. So my father sheepishly asked a station agent, "How much will it cost for all of us to get to Lodz?" The agent, callous at first, but sympathetic after seeing us children, turned to my father and offered his services. He was so touched that our family had stayed together during the war that he charged my father a respectable price of 100 rubles and ushered us to a private cattle-car. Though we wouldn't have comfortable seats in a regular passenger car, there was enough space for all eight of us. I have to admit it felt better than living in a cave during the previous two winters. So we took the train from Vilna to Lodz, and from there, we had to find our way behind American or British lines in Germany.

The trip to Lodz wasn't smooth. At the end of the first day's travel, the train stopped moving for the duration of a night. When Pop went to discover the cause of the stoppage, he was told that it was a planned stop. "Let's go," he insisted. "We are on the wrong train." It turned out that he had to pay more money to get us lodging for the night and secure passage on the correct train. We spent the night in the home of a local. I don't think we ever learned the family's name. In the morning, when the sky turned a beautiful powder blue, with marshmallow clouds intermittently covering up the bright sun, we piled into another cattle car, confident we were now on the right track to Lodz.

Many hours later, we arrived at the Lodz refugee processing center. The refugee agents began sobbing when they saw us children enter their office. They leaped from their seats. "How did you do it? How did you keep your wife and children alive and together?" they expressively asked Pop. The processing attendants said that they had not seen any children walk into the refugee office since the war ended. The sight of us children was a miracle, they exclaimed.

Pop replied, "I didn't do it. It was God that saved the children. I only helped."

In Lodz, Pop learned that two of my Mom's nieces, Frieda, and Shura, whose mother had died in the Dachau concentration camp, survived the war and had registered at the Lodz refugee center. The girls were able to survive the camp because they were younger and able to prove their value by working as seamstresses. My mother desperately wanted to find her nieces. It took two weeks, but the agents were able to help my parents locate them.

There were now ten of us: the five in my immediate family, plus Aunt Henya and my cousin Lile, Aunt Basia, and now Frieda and Shura. Officials instructed us to travel to Berlin, which had been divided into four sectors, one each controlled by the Allies: the United States, Great Britain, France, and the Soviet Union. They insisted that we make it to the American sector of West Berlin. We were told, "The Russian soldiers were inflicting revenge on the German people. Anyone in the Soviet zone would be at risk." The Soviets were taking spoils by robbing the people of valuables, especially jewelry. They had also become notorious for assaulting defenseless and vulnerable women. Even after the war, Berlin remained a war zone. It was no place for children. It was no place for a Jewish family that had just survived 18 months in the wilderness. From the American zone, however, we might find our way to Israel or perhaps to the United States. The irony of it all was too much. We were now destined to the country that was responsible for taking away our livelihood and for making us refugees.

The people in Lodz did not tell us how to get to Berlin. While stuck in the city for the two previous weeks, my father took notice of Russian trucks that traveled to and from Berlin pretty regularly. He set out to induce someone to drive us there. Using persuasion and bribes, my father ended up finding a Russian soldier that accepted vodka to drive us to Germany's capital city. We were dropped off at the edge of Berlin, where we walked the remainder of the way through the city's rubble to the American sector.

It was eerie walking through the city. I thought to myself: these were the people that turned a blind eye to their country's war crimes. How was it that we were now wandering through the streets without a sign of justice for us? Even if Nazism was defeated, anti-Semitism was still a lingering epidemic, I was sure. It was particularly unnerving to see very few adult men in the city. The surviving elderly men, women, and children were in a weakened condition that I had a sense of hopelessness for them.

American soldiers in Berlin were a godsend for us. They were obviously overwhelmed, trying to deal with countless war refugees. Nevertheless, they did what they could for my family. We were given a small allotment of food. We were also escorted to a bombed-out apartment building that became our home for the next month. They supplied us with blankets, gloves, and jackets to help us keep warm. At times, the Americans aided Pop with his daily trips to sell whiskey, tobacco, and other items in the black market all over East Germany.

I have good memories of our interactions with the Americans in Berlin. On the contrary, what I recall about the Russians is not as pleasant. When it became more apparent that the Soviet Union's relationship with the Americans was growing dysfunctional, Pop sought advice from the American soldiers about our safety. He was told that our family would remain intact and safe if we could make it to Bavaria, the American sector in Southern Germany, where several displaced persons camps had been constructed in urban centers like Munich. That was enough for my father. By winter 1946, he informed all of us that we were moving. The ten of us packed up our belongings, boarded a train at Postdamer Bahnhoff—which was no small task considering much of the station lay in ruin—and continued our nomadic journey to Munich.

CHAPTER 16

AFTER **A** **TRAIN** journey through high mountains and dark
forests, we arrived among huddled masses in Munich. The city
was overwhelmed by refugees. Many were Jews that had been liberated
from concentration camps and those like us who went into hiding.
Most, however, were German citizens that lost their homes in the
Allies' strategic bombing in the final months of the war. No one said
much of anything as we held one another's hands and maneuvered our
way through the crowds of disheveled people in the streets.

My father got us assigned to a camp in the village of Wolfratshausen,
about 17 miles south of Munich, called Fohrenwald. Ours was the
largest of all the Displaced Persons camps in Bavaria. Hitler originally
constructed Fohrenwald as a planned labor community for chemical
and munitions workers. Now, this assembly center existed as our life-
line, as General Eisenhower declared it a camp exclusively for Jews.
This decision made Fohrenwald a Jewish state within Germany. It was
a practical replacement for my *shtetl* back in Myadel. Fohrenwald was
known then and still is today, as the epicenter for the cultural revival
of my people. Indeed, a mesh wire fence surrounded the camp. That
fence, however, did not prevent any of us from traveling outside camp-
grounds at any time. We had virtual autonomy to come and goes as
we pleased. Inside the barriers, the adults were allowed to publish their

own newspapers, to pursue entrepreneurial enterprises, and engage in private elections for the purpose of forming a camp government that would champion the interests of DPs in the camp. The children would eventually have opportunities to play competitive sports, to form social clubs and theater groups, to attend schools, and perform musical instruments of our choosing.

Since Fohrenwald originally existed as a communal work village, it was not constructed like poorly insulated military barracks of other DP Camps in Germany. Many of the buildings in Fohrenwald were row houses. And when the Americans first arrived, the streets in Wolfratshausen were renamed after the states in the United States of America. The ten of us were placed on the second floor of a building on 21 Indiana Street. It appeared big from the outside. But inside, the space was small. We were given cots to sleep on and blankets to keep us warm. The floor was hard. There was some furniture, curtains, central heating, and a traditional kitchenette. A windowless but private communal latrine was on the floor beneath us. It had a toilet. It also had a bucket that we were supposed to use to bath. And so began our stay at the Fohrenwald Displaced Persons Camp.

Outside, boys and girls of all ages who survived the worst conditions were now running, playing, and laughing without a care in the world. I hadn't seen children in years! We didn't see any children in Myadel after the war. And in my month in Berlin, I couldn't recall seeing any children. It felt triumphant being in Fohrenwald. The bliss radiated by the children, and the breeze in the moist air made for an almost out-of-body experience. When I saw women with babies and children my age playing, I didn't have to think much about the horrors of the three previous years. Though I wasn't in the Jewish Land of Palestine, like Pop had spoken about for many months now, I was among people who shared my emptiness. Our new lives at Fohrenwald offered a sense of regenerated innocence.

Under the leadership of Mariam Warburg, Fohrenwald provided schools for the children. Miss Warburg spearheaded the recruitment of our teachers. She found resources for us. And she supervised the

curriculum. Her job was no easy task, especially since she was deal-
ing with a heterogeneous group of students that arrived at Fohrenwald
from places all over Europe. We were instructed by Israeli teachers that
spoke only Hebrew. This made learning challenging. The kids spoke
all types of languages. Among the displaced were Poles, Slavs, French,
Hungarians, Russians, Germans, Belarusians, and Lithuanians. Each
spoke their native tongue. Then there were those like my brothers and
me who spoke Yiddish. Although hardly any of us understood Hebrew,
we were required to speak it to the teachers. To their credit, the teachers
were patient with us, using hand gestures and some Yiddish words to
communicate. The whole school system at Fohrenwald was geared to
preparing us to move to Palestine (later-Israel). That included classes in
grammar, arithmetic, religion, and music.

An additional challenge to our education was how students were
divided into classes. The teachers placed us in school according to our
age, not our ability. Like our languages, our backgrounds in education were too distinct. Many of us had no formal schooling. Each day,
nevertheless, we pressed on. What we had gone through during the
war had everything to do with our discipline and positivity as Miss
Warburg made adaptations each and every day.

I had one friend that helped me pass the time each day. She was
from Poland. By the end of my three years at Fohrenwald, I was fluent
in Polish. At first, however, we communicated through smiling and
nodding. Sometimes she drew me a picture then pronounced the word
in Polish. I would repeat the annunciation. What made us good friends
at the start was that we had a similar interest when it came to music.
We both wanted to play the piano. So our parents signed us up for
piano lessons.

Our piano tutor was a German woman that lived outside the camp.
Together, we would ride our bikes through Wolfratshausen to rehearsal.
There were times when we encountered anti-Semitic bullies on our
way. The German kids in town would stand on the side of the road
and throw stones at us. *Farfluchte Yude!* They would yell. "Damned,
Jew!" It was in those moments that our new lives would get interrupted

with thoughts of past tragedies. I could only imagine what my father experienced at work every time he journeyed out of the camp.

Pop was involved in selling food and other items in the black market. The German people were undergoing obvious depravity after the war. Even though the German government, under the control of the American Military Government-authorized rations stamps to German citizens, the people still lived hand-to-mouth. Many were worse off. As a result, a large black-market operation undertaken by Germans, Jews, and some American soldiers was widespread in Germany. It seemed, however, that Jews were the only ones that took the brunt of the criticism. Indeed, every cross-section in Germany was doing it. My father was more or less involved in bartering with ration items for things the people personally needed. He often traveled to Munich to do his work. As a DP, Pop received items like Hershey's chocolate, clothing, and cigarettes from the Americans. These items were unavailable to the German population. He readily sold or traded those items to the Germans. He realized he was engaging in illegal activity, but given what he had suffered at the hands of the Germans, he could not understand the dishonesty of it all. After all, after he lost his fortune in the war, he was saving up money for our departure from the DP camp. A combination of the level of competition in the black market and lingering stereotypes of the Jew as a haggler who was incapable of obtaining a real occupation, my father was often a target of anti-Semitic rants. The Americans protected my father and others that worked in the black market by preventing the German police from entering Fohrenwald to make arrests or to seize the goods. This added to the tension between the German officials and the American occupation army. It also fostered the prejudices that Germans held toward us. It made us ever vigilant every time we traveled into Wolfratshausen.

My parents were always preemptive in making us feel at home despite the occasional combative experiences with the townspeople. They were big in pushing our cultural rehabilitation through social activities. They encouraged us to participate in camp activities that often evoked dreams of future life in Israel. In addition to playing the piano, I was interested in watching my peers sing and act on the stage. I was part of the camp's sports club called "Maccabi Jewish Gymnastics and Sports Club." The club saw to it that we had enough games to play year-round, including my favorites track and field and gymnastics. Annually, the camp would hold a sports festival that included among ten events the rope climb, broad jump, and sprinting. It was my favorite event of the year. It was equivalent to the Olympics' decathlon. When I was thirteen, I won! I was awarded a gold medal called the "Hamlu." Today, the Hamlu is one of my most prized possessions.

My brother, Chaim Zelman, was one of the better soccer players in the camp for his age group. He even participated in the camp's team that competed in a Jewish DP Camp soccer league made up of many teams from throughout all of the DP camps.

The American soldiers, of course, helped us obtain equipment and transportation to inter-camp cultural events.

CHAPTER 17

ONE OF THE most memorable days in Fohrenwald was May 14, 1948. I was 12 years old and sitting inside my classrooms when the principal interrupted the lesson to announce that Israel had been established as a state. Teachers throughout the building turned on their radio sets so we could listen to the broadcast announcing the end of the British mandate over the region and the establishment of the State of Israel. Proclamations were issued that invited Jews everywhere to become part of the new state. It was a celebratory occasion as all of the students were given little Israeli blue and white flags, lined up in pairs, and marched throughout the camp singing the *Hatikvah,* the Israeli national anthem. Now that immigration to Israel was legalized, the decommissioning of all but one DP camp soon followed.

Fohrenwald was the only DP camp still in operation after 1948. My cousins Frieda and Shura were soon married. They left with their new husbands for Israel. I was happy for them, but it was a sad departure. They were much older than me. I felt an extra boost of confidence every time they let me tag along with them to social gatherings. Then my Aunt Henya got married. She also left for Israel. Aunt Basia married too. She eventually resettled with her husband in Israel. My cousin Lile moved in with relatives in France before finally settling in Israel. Before long, our family shrunk from ten to the five of us: my parents, two brothers, and me.

That is how it was in the camp. During our three years at Fohrenwald, the rate of marriages and childbearing increased each year exponentially. The effort to extend families through both marriage and childbirth had much bearing on the conscious and unconscious effort to suppress the heavy emotional burdens of the past. Additionally, there was a shared desire by most in the camp to relocate to the Jewish Land, a physical and spiritual location among people that shared survivors' guilt.

The departure of my aunts and cousins combined with the resettlement of most of the camp's teachers, thespians, musicians, and camp administrators created a cultural vacuum at Fohrenwald. It all made me yearn to relocate to Israel more. Though it would not close until 1957, there were rumors that Fohrenwald would shut down in the summer of 1949. This would later be dispelled since so many sick and physically disabled Jewish DPs were still living in the camp. Additionally, many DPs from other camps that had not indicated a country in which they wished to resettle were transferred to Fohrenwald. Nonetheless, an instinct that I shared with my parents was that we would be forced to leave at some point. Perhaps in the Jewish Land, I could sustain my Fohrenwald experience of immersion in Jewish life and culture. It seemed right.

Always conscious of our safety, Pop and Mom were more cynical about going to Israel. A year earlier, thousands of Jewish immigrants, many were Holocaust survivors, onboard the *SS Exodus 1947* sailing for Israel (then-Palestine) from the Port de Sète near Marseille, France were arrested by the British and placed into refugee camps in Europe. My father was appalled by the news of how these refugees were treated. He feared that tensions lingered in the region regardless of the declaration of Israeli statehood. Moreover, Israeli tensions with the Arab League quickly escalated into war. The new Israeli capital Tel Aviv was peppered with bombs within two weeks of gaining statehood. "I didn't save my family during the war so they could die in Israel," he always said.

We had another option: America.

CHAPTER 18

IT WAS A Sunday morning in late May 1948. I slept in a little later than normal until the aroma of mother's tea compelled me to get a start on the day. When I greeted my parents at the kitchen table, they were discussing options for moving. Determined that Israel was too dangerous for us children, they debated moving anywhere from Australia to Canada. Then like a bee sting, a thought came to my Mom.

"I have family in America!"

When my mother was a child in Vilna, she spent most of her time with a cousin named David Schwab. The way my mother tells the story is that the two were inseparable as adolescent children. Whether they were attending Synagogue or playing in the street, the two were joined at the hip. She forgot about him all this time because they had not seen one another since they were very young. To escape the Russian pogroms under Czar Nicholas II, David's father left for America, leaving the family with my grandmother's family. The Schwab and my mother's families lived together in the same house until David's father earned enough money to call for them. That was before the outbreak of the First World War.

"How will we ever contact them?" Mom asked, a little annoyed.

Pop explained that they had a sense of where the Schwab family had once settled in the United States. The latest word on the Schwabs, albeit it was decades-old information, was that they were living in Binghamton, New York. He suggested that they send a letter addressed for David Schwab to the YMCA in Binghamton. Even if David was no longer living there, Pop suggested, there would have to be someone who once knew him and could forward our letter to his current address.

"The odds of connecting with them aren't good," he said, "but it is worth a shot."

Though we obviously didn't know this yet, most of the Schwabs were gone from Binghamton. Some, like David, had moved to Baltimore, Maryland, where they owned a family business called D&H Distributing Company.

My mother set out immediately to write the letter. With help from the American guards at Fohrenwald, she obtained the address for the YMCA in Binghamton, where she sent the note. It was post-marked to David Schwab, who was not a member of the YMCA. The branch executive noticed the name "Schwab" because there was an Abe Schwab that regularly attended the YMCA. The letter eventually fell into the hands of Abe, who was David's brother. The letter was written in Yiddish, which no one in Binghamton knew how to speak. Abe then contacted his brother, David, in Baltimore. He informed David of the letter and asked that they meet in Harrisburg, Pennsylvania, where their sister Anna, resided. In Harrisburg, the Schwabs had the letter translated by David Silver, the rabbi of Harrisburg's Kesher Israel Synagogue. A few weeks later, Mom and Pop heard back from the Schwabs. They informed us that they were taking all necessary precautions to sponsor us for entry to America.

I thought I had a healthy grasp on the linked fate of Jewish people across the world. This episode, however, opened my eyes to how tightly woven the global Jewish population was. Though geographically spread out, there was a sense that we were all neighbors, willing, and able to help one another through difficult times.

We were afraid that the immigration process would be very slow. Still in place in America were quota restrictions dating back to the 1920s that limited the number of immigrants coming to America from

Eastern Europe. Our saving grace was a temporary measure passed by the United States Congress and signed into law by President Truman near the end of 1948 called the Displaced Persons Act. For a short period of time, the law authorized thousands of displaced persons like us into the United States for permanent residence. My family was eligible for DP visas because the law stipulated that any victim of the Nazi war machine that was "detained or obliged to flee persecution from Nazi perpetrators" was considered eligible for admission into the United States given that someone already living there could testify that the refugees are law-abiding and hard-working people. The Schwabs had to ensure the government that we had a place to live in America, that we could hold jobs, and that we would become honest and patriotic citizens. We had to act quickly, however, as the government was only giving out 200,000 visas a year.

From thousands of miles across the Atlantic Ocean, the Schwabs helped change our immigration status. They provided the government with the necessary verification of how they would be responsible for our security. They were bringing us to America!

CHAPTER 19

BEFORE WE WERE allowed to go anywhere, we had to pass a physical exam, which included mental tests as well as an eye exam, chest X-rays, and blood work. While convincing immigration officials that we would be self-sufficient residents in the United States was David Schwab's most important job to handle in America, here in Fohrenwald, we had to prove to American officials that we were healthy enough to enter the country. We had to prove we were physically able to make the journey and that we wouldn't bring infectious diseases into the United States. This was a nerve-wracking experience.

The health examination took place in Fohrenwald. At the infirmary, my mother and I were taken into a room with other women and told to undress. I was insecure about standing naked in the public eye. I stood there, arms crossed firmly against my chest, legs tight, motionless like a statue. The American doctors and nurses tried to make all of us comfortable, but the cold and dim setting in the corridor left me in a state of discomfort. There was nothing they could do or say that would make me feel relaxed.

There was an endless wait to see the doctor. The line moved slowly. I shivered. Then inched ahead. I shivered some more. Then inched ahead some more. Mom spoke to me during our wait. But I kept shivering. I kept inching forward. The wait was psychological torture.

Ahead of us was a desk, behind it was a doctor. As each woman reached this point, she gave her name and then stood in silence as the doctor performed the examination. I arrived in front of a doctor ahead of Mom. He spoke to me in English, which I hardly understood. It didn't matter, however. It took only a minute, as he looked me over and then sent me to the next station to get a chest X-ray. Mom explained that the X-ray was to take a close look at my lungs. The Americans were worried that sick refugees might cause a tuberculosis outbreak in America. Before we entered Fohrenwald in the winter of 1946, there had been a TB epidemic that sickened almost 400 people. Though I never got sick with TB during our three years at the camp, I was concerned that the time I fell deathly ill while in the forest was indeed tuberculosis. I was in a state of panic. I might be the reason why my family didn't make it to America. But when the X-ray results were read, they showed I had no problems with my lungs. My mother, on the other hand, had received unexpected bad news. She was diagnosed with cataracts.

Her first reaction was to tell Pop to go on to America without out her. "Take the children and go," she said.

Pop just shook his head. "No, that's not what we are going to do," he replied. What he did next was classic Pop. "Come," he said, grabbing Mom by the arm. "We will go talk to the doctors." He promised all of us were going to America.

Pop and Mom acquired a translator before arriving at the infirmary. Maybe the doctors took pity on them because they had three children, but by the end of their conversation, the doctors determined that Mom's disease was not contagious. My parents were told that all of us would be allowed to go to America.

From Fohrenwald, we traveled north to the North Sea Port of Bremerhaven. The journey onboard a passenger train was long, but it was filled with fellow Holocaust survivors all going to America. Every person on the train, it seemed, was damaged and in need of one another to recover. We now found the promise of a new home on the uppermost in every mind. We were headed toward a new world that allowed us to start our lives over in a good way.

In Bremerhaven, we boarded the *USS General W. M. Black*. In one sense, I was giddy boarding the ship. I had only sailed on a boat once before. It was for a summer camp trip with Fohrenwald displaced persons along the Rhine River. I loved that experience very much. In another way, I was intimidated. The ship was enormous, and only it was not a passenger ship but a naval transport vessel. As we were unloading our things from the train onto *General Black*, the men were separated from the women. The women were at the front of the ship and the men in the rear. The sleeping quarters were in the bowels of the boat. We were given cots to sleep on. The women's room was very large and very crowded.

General Black departed Bremerhaven about two o'clock on March 26, 1949. After sailing for a few hours, I overhead some people saying that the ship had a planned stop in London, England. Naturally, I joined everyone on deck to see the famous city. I was very disappointed, however, because all I could see were lights and not enough of the city to suit me. Nevertheless, I was thrilled to be able to say that I saw London.

The next day everyone went to the cafeteria to eat; there was a lot of food for everyone, and I could eat as many oranges and lemons as I pleased. In the afternoon, we went on deck, and everyone felt fine. Before long, people started to get seasick. Indeed, I did not feel too well, either. In the evening, it was very cold on deck, but as soon as I went downstairs to our cabin, I started to get dizzy and sick. All I could do about it was to eat more oranges and lemons. Even that didn't help much.

It was an uncanny feeling being surrounded by water with no land in sight. As the days passed, I would wander on deck to watch the birds flying around. I wished that I could be one of them. They looked so happy and free. They could do anything. They could go anywhere they wished. At that time, all I could think of was "land." I prayed every morning and every night before I went to bed.

One day the captain announced that he wanted everyone on deck to wear our lifesaver belts. I really felt as if it were the end of my life, but it turned out to be only a practice drill. Everybody moved quickly and quietly to his or her stations with sincerity. This drill was for a good reason. Just a few days later, everyone on the boat faced a huge scare.

On April 1, the captain said that our ship was going to hit bad weather. That evening no one was allowed on deck. As I sat on my bed and looked around at all the people, I could see their pale faces. Many were very sick. Others were just plain scared. Young children who never had a worry in their lives were saying, "I hope my mommy gets better" or "I wish I could be in a house now." I didn't feel so well myself, and I couldn't say much to help ease the situation. About midnight, the storm struck with all its force, and the ship began to rock to and fro. All the people started to pray and walk around the corridor. The waves were so high, they splashed over the deck, and the water started to come in my room. I could hardly wait until daylight because with dawn, as I had hoped, the storm abated.

On this very day, the captain announced that tomorrow *General Black* would arrive in New York. By this time, the ship was moving along much steadier. Still not allowed on deck, I spent most of the day wondering what America would be like and anxious to see the Statue of Liberty about which my mother had mentioned so often. To me, America meant a new life that guaranteed freedom. It was a place free from the remnants of pure evil. In America, we would have privacy. We would have clean water. We would be able to live audaciously. We would be able to live without fear for the first time in our lives.

The next morning there was quite a commotion aboard when someone said, "I see land!" I skipped breakfast to go on deck with the others. As our ship drew closer to the Statue of Liberty, I could feel my heart begin to pound. I said to Mom, "Mother, I'm not scared anymore, and I don't mind being sick for a few days." In a sudden rush of adrenaline, I no longer felt sick. Like the masses, I felt joy. I felt free. Pop put his arm around Mom. They smiled at the sight of the statue. To this day, that moment, when I saw Lady Liberty is one of the most memorable experiences of my life.

CHAPTER 20

THE *GENERAL BLACK* docked first at Ellis Island, where we were processed. Our luggage was checked. The immigration agents steered us to a medical inspection. Though much faster, and fully clothed, this experience was just as frightening as it was in Fohrenwald. We were told to walk through the labyrinth of the immigration station's halls. Doctors looked for anyone short of breath during the walk, a sign of heart disease or physical abnormalities. We were then sprayed with disinfectant powder and directed to the first of two physical inspections. The first examiner did a preliminary examination to look for facial defects and lice. He looked for signs of ringworm on our skin. He used a stethoscope to listen to our hearts and lungs. The second doctor inspected our eyes. We had some concerns because of the diagnosis of Mom's cataracts prior to our departure. This doctor, however, was not concerned about cataracts. He was looking for trachoma, an eye disease that often led to death. We were a bit on edge because the word was that anyone found with the disease was to be sent back to Europe. We all passed that examination and were shepherded to a lower level where we found our luggage and waited to board a ferryboat to carry us to New York City.

I held Mom's hand as we waited for the transport ship to take us to Manhattan. I was staring down at the wooden floor when I heard a voice shouting, "Is that you, Reva?" It was David Schwab. Mom let go of my hand and hugged him as tears welled up in her eyes. David was there with another cousin of my mother's, Sam Dimentstein. My eyes were fixated on the two men. All of us were in rags compare to the tailored suits they were wearing. This wasn't something I thought about until this moment. Like a natural 13-year-old girl, I felt insecure. "You must be hungry," David said, looking in my direction. Then looking back at Mom, he said we would get something to eat when we reach New York City. He also told us he made arrangements for us to sleep comfortably in the city before taking us to his sister's house in Harrisburg, Pennsylvania, where he arranged for us to live.

In a few hours, we finally docked at the pier in Manhattan. In New York, I was amazed at what I saw; the bridges, the paved streets, the incalculable number of cars motoring throughout the city. I steered my gaze on the people. That night we slept in the Edison Hotel. Well, my family slept. I was up all night watching the lights outside my window. I remember taking a long and private bath for the first time in my life. My first hours on American soil gave me the feeling that I was now as free as the birds that flew over the *General Black*.

CHAPTER 21

BY THE END of April, we moved into the home of David Schwab's sister, Anna, in Harrisburg, Pennsylvania, while David remained in Baltimore. Anna and her husband, Sam Kleiman, were gracious hosts in spite of us intruding on their privacy, consuming their food, and otherwise disrupting their lives. With their help, our lives immediately started to change. My father started work at the Harrisburg branch of the Schwabs' family business, D&H Distributing, located on the 300 block of South Cameron Street, a major access road that ran through Harrisburg and operated as the local Radio Corporation of America distributor. Mom remained home to help Anna with household needs. My parents also attended night school to learn English. They did this for at least a year. I remember watching them read the evening news as they tussled with headlines and columns. They often quizzed one another on what each word meant.

The best clue of where my family's lives would lead occurred at one of our first dinners, held at the home of David Schwab's son, Morris, whom we affectionately called "Morrie," and his wife, Leona. Joining us at the dining table was the entire Schwab family, including son Izzy and his wife Elaine, and daughter Reva, and her husband, Julius. Of course, David and his wife Rachel were present. The dividing line between the Schwabs, a Jewish American family, and us, Jewish war refugees, was a fitting one for our arrival to the United States when the nation rested at the precipice of challenging its citizens and foreigners over loyalty. Reva, a woman known for her self-assertion and command of the room, gave us new names. It was a peculiar moment, but none of us seemed to have a problem with it. The McCarthy era was just months away. I would soon learn that this inaugural interfamily dinner was only an auspicious beginning to my life maneuvering the American social and political landscape.

"You all need American names," Reva precipitously said. I thought, what made her the authority? Eventually, I discovered that everyone looked up to Reva. She had style and confidence. I grew to admire her like I had my cousins in the DP camp. She changed Pop's name from Hendel to Henry. Chaim became Harold. Nochum was renamed Norman. Appropriately, she chose to keep my mother's name since it was the same as hers. As for me, I was christened Linda. To my peers, I was Linda Swidler (formerly Svidler), the transplanted one from Belorussia.

Only weeks after arriving in the United States, I enrolled in the seventh grade at Camp Curtain Junior High School. Neither my brothers nor I could speak a word of English. We were placed in school according to our ages, not our ability. I was 14 years old, and my brothers, now known as Harold and Norman, were 16 and 12, respectively. There was only a month remaining in the school year when we enrolled. I had trouble making friends during those weeks. I nevertheless tried and hoped to be accepted by my peers.

Other than Americanizing my name and locking myself in my home, there was little I could do those first few weeks in Harrisburg to help me feel comfortable in my environment. I seldom felt like an outsider, and people were very friendly to me. And yet, there was a feeling inside me that gave me a sense of alienation. I remember one student offering to read a Dr. Seuss book to me. Others tried to teach me the alphabet. It made me happy that there were thoughtful people at Camp Curtain that made an effort to make me feel comfortable. Still, I recall feeling like everyone around me was always staring. I never felt like other people looked at me as a problem; they just saw me as unusual, obviously foreign, and culturally awkward. I went to school each day feeling like I was the Other. I was the outsider that seemingly existed as an exhibit on display for everyone to gawk at.

The burden of isolation—granted, not racial but linguistic polarization—contrasted with my predetermined image of the American dream. While onboard the *General Black,* I envisioned America as the land where I would escape tragedy and not have to worry that my religion or my family's history might cause harm to anyone in my family or me. I admit, before we arrived in America I thought little about how I would fit in with children my own age. I saw the country as a haven for freedom. I envisioned the United States as a sun shining down on me during a spring day. My experience at Camp Curtain Junior High told me otherwise.

When the school year concluded, a miracle happened that changed my whole life as an American teenager. David Schwab's wife, Rachel, was traveling to Williamsport, Pennsylvania, to visit with her mother. Harrisburg was on the way, so she stopped to see us at the Kleimans'. She asked whether I wanted to join her for the two-and-a-half-hour drive north of Harrisburg.

"Of course," I said. "Yes! Yes!" Even though she couldn't speak Yiddish and I hardly understood English, I was so ecstatic to join Rachel to see more of the American countryside.

While visiting with her mother, Rachel took me across the street to play with the kids of their neighbors. The Snowiss family was welcoming. They had three children—Leo, Faye, and Susan—who were about my age. Communicating with one another was difficult, but we used our childhood instincts to find games to play that did not involve much speaking. My favorite game that day was hide-and-seek. I had never played it before. Such a simple game that entailed both outwitting and outrunning my new friends gave me so much joy.

Playing with Leo, Faye, and Susan was so much fun that I cried when Rachel returned to get me. I wanted to stay there forever. She saw the anguish in my eyes and took action. She made arrangements with my parents and the Snowiss' to allow me to stay in Williamsport for half of the summer. Everyone agreed. I stayed with them for six weeks. During that time, I learned English and lost my accent. All it took was a summer playing with the Snowiss'. I just loved that summer. The friendship I developed with Fay, in particular, was the best thing that happened to me. It has been 60 years since we first met. We have always remained good friends.

Though we would officially become citizens in May 1957, it was my summer with the Snowiss' when I finally felt like an American. I believe today that I could probably be an ambassador for the United States because of how much I love America.

Most of my life experiences gave me an ear for picking up languages. At home, we spoke only Yiddish. I heard Belarusian, Russian, Polish, and Hebrew in Pop's dry good store. Before the war, my nanny, Paluta, spoke Belarusian. In the DP camp, I was inundated with foreign languages. There are obvious differences between Slavic and Western European Romance languages. My friends in the DP camp and I used to make fun of English. "Put a hot potato in your mouth, and you will sound like that too," the kids at Fohrenwald often said. And yet, I knew Americans spoke English. My short time with the Snowiss family reassured my confidence in picking up any language that I encountered. It also restored confidence in my idea of America.

At the end of the summer, I looked for work. My first job was as a babysitter for David Schwab's son, Morris, and his wife Leona, who possessed a keen interest in flowers. Morris, who was 30 years old in 1949 and whom I would later call "Morrie," a graduate of Penn State and general manager at the Harrisburg branch of the Schwab family business D&H Distributing Company, offered to pay me a small stipend to watch their four children when they went out for dinner or a movie on the weekends. Their children, Richard, Jimmy, Andy, and Betsy, took to me right away. I shared the feeling. Years later, apart from my children, Morrie would later become the most important person in my life. In addition to paying me to babysit his children, and unbeknownst to my brothers and me, he purchased a house for my family. By way of secret deal-making, Mom and Pop moved us out of the Kleiman house and into our own home in the northern end of the city. Morrie had purchased the property and told my father to pay him monthly payments. It would be decades before I discovered this unselfish act. The house was a charming two-story, three bedrooms, and one bathroom brick row home with a small yard.

The Schwabs then referred me to family friends, Donnie Freedman, a doctor at the city hospital, and his wife, Myrl. The Freedmans were a Jewish family that lived about 15 minutes away from my neighborhood, Jefferson Village. They provided me with a bicycle and gave me free lessons in English in addition to the allowance I received for watching their kids. I babysat at the Freedmans' for years. We became good friends throughout my life.

In addition to work, my improved English afforded me new friends when my eighth-grade year at Camp Curtain Junior High commenced. Helen Isachman, Elain Katz, and Norma Freedberg were Jewish-Americans with a fine understanding of what it was like to be Jewish and live in the United States. They helped me fit in at school. Norma's father and mother would often have me read books to them. It was an opportunity for me to work on my English. Another friend, Sandy Camp, who I met in eighth-grade gym class where we were forced to march around to John Philip Sousa's "The Stars and Stripes Forever" and other military songs, convinced me to get involved in every extracurricular offered at school. We joined a group in the school marching band called "The Swingerettes." We were majorettes with a catchy nickname. We participated in many forms of athletics that were available to women in 1949 and 1950. Sandy's mother was also helpful as she found ways for me to practice English at times when I was at their family restaurant.

In September 1951, over two years since our arrival in the United States, I started tenth grade at William Penn High School, a senior high school in uptown Harrisburg. After two years spent trying to acquire an identity at junior high, I had become one of the more popular girls in my class. I had dated my first boyfriend in ninth grade. By the time I enrolled in high school, I was on a date most weekends. My parents didn't seem to mind. They allowed me to date because I never abused the curfew they imposed. I was very responsible. I dated mostly Jewish suitors. And while most of the men I dated were near my age, I occasionally went out with college students from nearby Dickinson College that often visited the Jewish Community Center in Harrisburg on weekends. My parents never thought to arrange a courtship. This may have been because we were in the United States.

It didn't matter anymore that I was a refugee. And I never had to deal with anti-Semitism in Harrisburg schools. I had become involved in a multitude of extracurricular activities at school that helped aid in my growing popularity. I attended football games, which was and still is a big deal in Harrisburg. I was a member of a championship soccer team, played volleyball, ping-pong, tennis, badminton, and basketball at William Penn. I was also chosen to be a flag spinner in the color guard at high school. Because of my grades and athleticism, my teachers nominated me to become an executive member of the all-girls society known as "Siminar," the high school's student activities organization. Ten girls per class, or 30 total, were selected to essentially govern the whole school. It is peculiar to think of it today, but our job in Siminar was to be party-planners that organized all the intramural sports. It was a duty that enabled us women to control the social lives of nearly everyone at William Penn. The 30 of us were in charge of planning the school's social events. In particular, we had to organize the school's Friday night scruff dances.

It helped that I had become a socialite by tenth grade. I was very pretty at the time. I had dark black hair, a nice figure, and an alluring charm that seemingly made me a catch among single Jewish and Christian men. At scruff dances, I regularly danced with men taller than me. They would put me on a chair and dance with me. We would do the "Jitter Bug" or the "Charleston." The weekend dances were so much fun, though I often received jealous stares from other girls in the auditorium.

I often went with friends—with my parents' permission, of course—to fraternity weekends at Penn State College, later Penn State University. I was also in the school choir. When I joined, I asked Pop if it was all right that I sing "Jesus songs."

"Why not? Go ahead," he approved.

In eleventh grade, my peers at the Jewish Community Center voted me "Sweetheart" of the Aleph Zadik Aleph Fraternity, an organization for Jewish teenagers. The honor suggested that I had become the "true American girl," at least among those at William Penn High School and the City of Harrisburg. Mom was so proud that she threw a party for me. It was the only time I remember her spending money on a party.

I often think back to those high school days of mine. Only in America, I believed, could I have been involved in so much as a teenager. My time in Harrisburg was remarkable and exciting; to learn and mingle with people of different backgrounds was analogous to my experience at the DP Camp, only that in Harrisburg I didn't live with uncertainty about my family's future. The hardships of the war had become a distant memory as I matured and grew older. My experiences at Camp Curtain and William Penn, in addition to the benevolent support from my parents, helped me overcome reminders of those trying times during the war.

I wrote an essay during my junior year about "what freedom meant to me." I won first prize and received a $50 War Bond. The essay moved my English teacher so much so that she sent it to the local newspaper, the *Patriot-News*. The newspaper called me "an inspiration to everyone." It added, "She will always be remembered not only as the sweetheart of the AZA but also as a true example of a typical American girl." I received an invitation from the State Assembly because of the publication asking me to read my essay in the Senate Chambers at the Pennsylvania Capitol. My presentation was broadcasted live on public television. I got through it despite how nervous I was. I remember barely being able to get the words out.

My free time as a teenager was spent at the newly constructed Jewish Community Center on the north end of Harrisburg. It was at the JCC where, during my senior year, I met my future husband. I was with a group of girlfriends when I spotted a tall, trim, and mature young man playing basketball. His name was Edward "Eddie" Rubin.

Eddie was six years older than me. He came from a big family. His father, Aaron, was an immigrant. His mother, Lena, was born in the United States. He had four siblings: his older sister, Anne; Louie, who died in a car accident many years earlier; Bobby, who had served in the Battle of Okinawa; and his youngest sister, Ellie. Like his brother Bobby, Eddie had spent time in the service. He served in the Korean War after graduating from William Penn High School, class of 1948. He shined on William Penn's basketball team when he was a student, where they called him "Captain Ed." He had a reputation for playing rough. This explains why he was also good at football despite the fact that his parents were adamant about how dangerous the game was. He also threw the javelin on William Penn's track and field team.

I was determined to introduce myself after his pick-up basketball game. Where did that confidence come from? Looking back, I am happy I made the first move! Who knows if we would have ever spoken to one another if I didn't approach him. We started dating instantly. Despite the age difference, my parents approved, as did his. Eddie took me to my senior prom. All the girls were jealous that I had a fetchingly sophisticated older date.

Golf became a hobby that connected us even closer together. Eddie and my brother Harold became good friends. Harold worked as a caddy at Blue Ridge Country Club, and he picked up the sport rather quickly. On his days off, Harold would take Eddie with him to play golf. Eddie loved it so much that he wanted me to learn. He wanted to make sure I had all the proper instruction, so he hired Bob Dunn, the Blue Ridge Country Club golf professional, to teach me the proper swing. I fell just as hard for the game as I did for Eddie. Later, when we had children, my friends teased me because I would rather sneak off to the golf course while my children napped to play a few holes.

After graduation in the spring of 1954, I applied to the Pennsylvania Business School in Harrisburg to obtain a degree in secretarial science.

My experience in college, however, was cut short when I broke my thumb getting out of Eddie's car. I haphazardly got it caught in the car door. Instead of taking me to the emergency room the moment I got my thumb jammed in the door, Eddie rushed me to the Freedmans' house where I babysat. Dr. Freedman cut the nail and sliced an X in my finger where the nail used to be in an attempt to let the blood escape and to release the pressure on my thumb. I had a bandage on my hand for several months. Any plans I had for a career in typing was over for the time.

Eddie said to me, "Well, Linda, why do we have to wait for you to get a job. Let's just get married now!"

"Okay!" I said. He took me directly to his house and gave me a beautiful ring. He had already planned to propose!

He said, "This is where we will live."

We were married in March 1955 in a small ceremony at his house. Only family was present. Rabbi of Kesher Israel Synagogue in Harrisburg, David Silver, and Moshe Orbach, the Cantor at Kesher Israel, officiated the wedding. I thought it was a beautiful wedding.

One year later, we had our first child, a daughter, Sandra Rose, or "Sandee." In 1958, our second was born, Adina Lee. We affectionately called her "Dini." While pregnant with our third child, a son, Stephen Alen, I was at the peak of my bowling career at the Jewish Community Center. I was tops in the Women's Division of the National Jewish Welfare Board's Bowling tournament. Our matches were on Tuesdays. "Don't worry," I told my teammates, "my son won't ever be born on a Tuesday, because that is league day." I gave birth to Stephen on a Thursday.

I stayed at home with the children while Eddie worked for his family's business, Rubin Bros. Co. Inc. Our children went to Hebrew school, or *Yeshiva*, which was supervised by Rabbi Silver. They then attended Susquehanna Junior High and Susquehanna Township High School. All three of our children were involved in multiple sports and volunteer activities. Sandee went on to become a dental hygienist. She obtained degrees from the University of Pennsylvania and New

York University. Sandee married a Dr. Joshua Greenberg, a periodontist. They settled near us in Harrisburg and had one daughter, Ellen Rae. Ellen worked as a teacher for the Philadelphia Schools with two Master's degrees. She was tragically murdered at the age of 26. A piece of my heart left me.

My second daughter Dini attended the University of Pennsylvania and received her Master's Degree in Business from George Washington University. She married a prosthodontist, Dr. Robert Sanker, and they lived in Maryland with their bright and beautiful daughters, Erica and Lauren.

My youngest son, Stephen, graduated from the University of Maryland and joined the family business. He married my wonderful daughter-in-law, Jennifer Serkin. They also have two beautiful and smart daughters, Ali and Caroline. Their third child was a boy, Edward Robert Rubin (Eddie's namesake). Edward died of Leukemia before the age of two.

CHAPTER 22

WHEN STEPHEN ENTERED high school, his father became sick with cancer. All three of his years at Susquehanna Township High School, he watched his father, Eddie, battle for his life.

Eddie was always a health freak. He had a proven track record as a high school sports star, war veteran, and local golf aficionado. But during a routine physical exam, his doctor found something concerning and sent him to Johns Hopkins Medical Center for a cancer screening. The doctor at Johns Hopkins diagnosed him with testicular cancer and ordered immediate surgery. Though precautionary, the surgery was a serious issue, and it left Eddie in prolonged pain. He was cut around his body as the doctor removed his Retroperitoneal lymph node. His recovery was an excruciatingly painful experience. I slept in a dorm room at the college so I could be there for him every waking moment.

Eddie never recovered to full health after the surgery. The doctor was very surprised and took his test results to Northeastern University. After a careful review, we were told that Eddie was misdiagnosed. Our doctor told us that Eddie was suffering from pancreatic cancer. Though we tried to stay positive, cancer had spread to new areas of the body. He didn't have long to live.

My dear Eddie passed away in 1980. He was 50 years old.

Our son, Stephen, was weeks away from graduating high school and starting the next phase of his life at the University of Maryland. For as hard as it was to cope with his death, Eddie had left me, Stephen. Stephen was a spitting image of his father. He walks like him, talks like him, and acts like him without even knowing. Every glance at Stephen, I saw Eddie.

I had trouble adhering to the traditional Jewish notion about death; that is, that death is not a tragedy but rather a part of the cycle of life. In *Shiva*, Jews traditionally mourn the loss of loved ones for a week. People come to visit during the mourning period. After that initial stage of bereavement, it is expected that those in mourning get back to their daily lives while wearing a black band or cut tie in remembrance of the departed. That is not how I dealt with Eddie's death. After his burial at Harrisburg's Chisuk Emuna Cemetery, I mourned him for a long period of time.

I played a lot of golf to help me mend. There were times I felt Eddie was out there with me. Since he loved golfing as much as I did, playing rounds actually filled the void in my life in a profound way. For many years, I spent little time with anyone who refused golf. It benefited me in a way. The whole experience actually made me a determined and resilient golfer.

I also started a distinguished competitive bridge career. I started playing bridge with a group of friends called "The Sunshine Girls." We learned the card game by joining a novice league at the Harrisburg Bridge Club on Tuesday nights. Before long, we began entering tournaments at the Host Resort in Lancaster, Pennsylvania.

My friend Bea Wolfe and I played in a National Bridge Tournament. We played in the KNOCKOUTS and were lucky enough to win the section.

I had obtained enough points to be considered a "Life Master" in that tournament. I am now a Bronze Life Master and Silver Life Master. As I write this memoir, I play against the best bridge players in the country at the Pompano Bridge Club.

On June 5, 1997, I was inducted into the Harrisburg Jewish Community Center Sports' Hall of Fame. My good friend De De Wolf presented me at the hall of fame ceremony. De De stated:

I am deeply honored and privileged to be standing here this
evening to speak about my dear friend, Linda Rubin Schwab. I am
sure that we all know that Linda was selected for this award because
of her outstanding ability on the golf course. However, I would
like to go back in time and tell you what an outstanding all-around
athlete she is.

The time, - 48 years ago, The place,-a D.P. camp in Germany, and
Linda is thirteen years old. Think about what it takes to win ALL
the evens, like today's decathlon. This thirteen-year-old won it all.
She won the "Hamlu." I am sure that many of you are wondering
what a hamlu is? Well, it is one of Linda's most prized possessions.
Let me show you this very "special" medal. This pin is equivalent
to our gold medal of today. Just think - at age thirteen - Linda had
already won the GOLD!

Shortly thereafter, Linda and the Swidler [sic] family came to this
country. And lucky for us, they settled in Harrisburg. She attended
junior and senior high school and did more in just a few years in
this country than most of us who were born here. These are just a
few of her accomplishments in high school. She was a member of a
championship soccer team, played volleyball, ping-pong, baseball,
tennis, badminton, and quoits,-all intramural sports. In addition,
she found time to sing in the school choir.

Now let us move to around thirty-five years ago to our then "new
JCC." A Tuesday morning bowling league. Linda carried between
a 160-168 average, and she had more 500 games accumulated
than any other person at that time at the JCC. She was tops in the
Women's Division of the National Jewish Welfare Board's 1961
Bowling Tournament. She rolled a 503. She was also pregnant with

Steve at the time. We knew that Steve would never be born on a Tuesday because that was league day. So he waited for a Thursday.

Eddie was the one who gave Linda the golf bug. He wanted to make sure that she had all the proper instruction. He hired Bob Dunn, the BRCC golf professional, to teach her the proper swing. Eddie encouraged her to practice. And practice she did. While the rest of us would get off our feet while the children were taking naps, not Linda. She got a sitter and flew off to the club to practice. And with only a short time before Sandee, Dini, and Steve would get up from their nap, she had grooved her way to the game of golf. The rest is history. Linda had all the right ingredients to become a champion. Determination, perseverance, the desire to win, and just plain, raw, talent. She has been the BRCC's Ladies Championship Golfer twelve times. Ed Tabor, who was quoted in the newspaper after he had followed Linda and Sandy Strock, said about her, and I quote, "She has the finest short game I have ever seen!" That was the year she had a 78 and was medalist in the Harrisburg Ladies District Tournament.

With all of this, Linda did something that many people with her credentials never do. She never forgot her friends. She set aside a day to play with everyone she could. I speak from experience. Monday was my special day. Does this have something to say about her character?

Her ability on the golf course is legendary. She is by far one of the best women golfers to come out of this area. All the hard work and practice has paid off. And would I like to say that Linda has given something back to the game of golf and to this entire community - and that word is "CLASS."

She is truly deserving of this honor, and it is my distinct honor to induct her into the Sports Hall of Fame. My friend, Linda Rubin Schwab.

What really did matter to me was being inducted into the Jewish Community Center's Hall of Fame with my first husband, Eddie, who was posthumously inducted for his high school feats in several sports. It was also a big deal for our children. The Jewish Community Center was a special place for us. It has always been a benignant organization that, over the years, has honored those who have sustained and represented the Jewish population in Central Pennsylvania. This was a deeply moving honor.

My two heroes, Pop and Mom, passed away shortly thereafter. They had spent a long life in America successfully managing a shoe shop in center-city Harrisburg. Pop died of a heart attack in 1988. Alone, Mom went to live with Norman, whose wife had suffered from MS and died a year earlier. Norman had two children that Mom and I helped raise. Eventually, Mom grew too sick to handle those responsibilities. We had her transferred to the Jewish Retirement Home of Greater Harrisburg. She lived there until she passed away in 1992 at the age of 92. Both of my parents were buried in Kesher Israel Cemetery, which is a burial place located near Chisuk Emuna Cemetery, where Eddie was laid to rest.

Mom and Pop were truly a pair in everything they did. The death of my parents occurred almost 50 years after we first went into hiding at the onset of World War II. Though the span of time between their bravery and heroism that kept us alive during the war and their death might make their passing seem inconsequential to the lives around them, their lives belong to a greater order of beings. They persisted in Belarus, Vilna, Germany, and the United States in the face of veiled and straightforwardly stated threats. It is easy for bystanders to look at tragedy and say they would step up. And yet, heroes are relatively rare. Indeed, most people envision themselves rushing to the aid of those in need. But unfortunately, rushing into danger is exceedingly impossible to do at the moment. This is why I believe Mom and Pop are exceptional. When the moment arose, they made all of the right decisions to keep my brothers and me alive. At every instant, they duped and defeated Nazi bureaucrats and Nazi soldiers that aimed to slaughter the

Jewish people. Pop literally took a bullet to save us. He lived on the run for days away from his family. He dug a cave and begged for food right under the noses of the Nazis. He tracked down one lost sister in the forest and another deep into the Soviet Union. He and Mom saved us from extinction. The thought of their resilience has helped me endure every hardship in my life.

CHAPTER 23

I WAS ALONE for almost three years after Eddie's death. While I mourned his passing, I felt no inner pang for companionship. I never had the urge to give any more of myself to anyone even though plenty of friends suggested I put myself back on the market. I was exhausted from taking care of my dear Eddie, the love of my life.

That changed in the summer of 1983. One day I was playing golf with my girlfriends, and my old friend Morrie Schwab was two holes ahead of us. He turned his cart around and asked me if I wanted tickets to see Liza Minnelli perform in Hershey. I didn't think twice. The daughter of Judy Garland and Vincente Minnelli and star of the film *Cabaret* was one of my favorite entertainers. "Yes!" I said without hesitation. That evening I accompanied Morrie to the show.

He later asked me to go to dinner. I felt it odd that this individual who was paramount in helping acclimate my family to live in the United States almost thirty years earlier was now asking me out. I admired Morrie for the active role he played in saving my family from the dangers of post-war Europe and for privately purchasing my family's first home in America. Additionally, he had become quite an accomplished individual. He was the CEO of Credential Leasing Corp while running his family's business, D&H Distributing, Co. He was also on the Board of Mellon Bank of Harrisburg. A graduate of

Penn State, '40, he was a sitting member on the university's Alumni Association. He was once awarded the United Jewish Communities of North America Endowment Achievement Award for his contributions to the Jewish Home of Greater Harrisburg, the Harrisburg Jewish Community Center, and for his role in creating the Holocaust Studies Chair at Penn State University's Harrisburg campus. I was puzzled when he asked me out a second time. He described the evening as casual. He explained all of his friends were taking their wives, and he needed a guest. So I joined him.

Morrie, too, had lost this spouse, Leona, to cancer a year after Eddie passed away. While I struggled to even look at another man for three years, he was much more cavalier in the way he handled the loss. The ladies were always after him. And he seemed to date them all. After all, he was just 65, and he hated being alone. He was always with someone. As a result, I had trouble taking his invitations seriously.

It was after our third night out that I realized we were dating. He took me to a business party sponsored by Harristown Enterprise Incorporated. Morrie sat on the company's board of directors. The affair was held inside a retail complex called Strawberry Square, located next to the Pennsylvania Capitol and only two blocks from the bank of the Susquehanna River. We danced and had a wonderful time. Too wonderful, I admit. I felt guilty that I was having such a good time with Morrie.

The next day, I traveled to Arizona with friends De De Wolf and Barbara Isaacman. While on the plane, I thought there was something wrong with me. If I were to meet this man in another city, I thought I would flip for him. And yet, he lives minutes away from me in Harrisburg. He was a nice-looking, single man, very gentleman-like, but I had trouble looking at him as something other than a family friend. Those feelings changed on that plane ride. The next time he called me I was excited to hear from him. I truly fell for him.

A few months after dating, he asked me to marry him. "I'm so much older than you," he said. He warned, "I will ruin your life. You could have someone much younger." I considered him a man of integrity. Even though he cared for me, he was realistic.

"I have no intention of looking for anyone else," I responded. I informed him that I must seek the approval from my children before giving him an answer. He was visibly irritated by that answer. Morrie's mother had died when he was very young. He initially did not want his father, David, to remarry. But when his father did, Morrie confessed that his stepmother, Rachel, was the best thing that ever happened to him. I guess he expected the same level of compliance from my children. "Just give me 10 good years, and I will be happy," I quipped.

"All right," he said. "Let's live each year as if it were five."

We had to find a date for our wedding, which was not an easy thing to do since Morrie was a very busy person. His daughter, Betsy, also carried a busy schedule. And so we looked through Morrie's little black book and found four days that both he and his daughter had available. We decided to get married when appropriate for Morrie's schedule.

We were married on December 23, 1983, in a ceremony officiated by my rabbi and Morrie's rabbi at the Chisuk Emuna Temple. Our honeymoon was local and untraditional. Betsy gave us her house for the night. She fixed up her bedroom like a honeymoon suite with flowers and candy. The next day, my daughter, Dini, and her husband, Bob, joined us to a ballet at the Kennedy Center in Washington, D.C. Betsy and her husband, Lou, joined us. The children put us up for the night at the famed The Georgetown Inn. It was a cold night, and the furnace inside the Georgetown was broken. The children had lots of laughs, thinking about how we were cuddling together to keep warm.

We returned to the Harrisburg Hilton for our first anniversary. Morrie sat on the Hilton's board. He was instrumental in the hotel's original construction in the capital city's downtown. Our party was like a Hollywood affair. We had a live band with lots of food and dancing. The children and friends provided entertainment.

Indeed, Morrie and I packed five years into every 365 days. The two of us traveled to Israel. Our favorite vacation destinations were Palm Springs and Lake Tahoe. Since Morrie was on the board of the Penn State Alumni Association for 18 years, we sat in the press box for all the home football games. We attended Penn State bowl games each New Year holiday. The two of us went to Scotland to play golf on a Penn State trip. We both enjoyed golf. During winters, we made it a habit to golf in Florida. We liked it so much that we eventually bought a house at Hunter's Run in Boynton Beach.

For most of my life, I was not comfortable talking about my experience during the Holocaust. I had nightmares, and I would wake up in a sweat, thinking it was happening now. I always told my parents I never wanted to talk about my past. I wanted to be an American and have friends. My past, I believed, was like a bad dream. After many people spent years urging me to tell my story, Morrie was the one who finally convinced me to record my story for the archives. It was time to talk about it. I first spoke to a group of school children in Harrisburg. They were studying the Holocaust, and the school wanted a survivor who could speak to the children. How could I say no? After all, I was their age when it all happened. I now regularly share my story with primary and secondary students. I explain to the children how important it is that I share my story with them. I challenge them to become Holocaust ambassadors with orders to convey my experiences to others after I am gone. I want them to say, "I met Linda Schwab."

It was because of Morrie that I later participated in Steven Spielberg's Shoah Foundation Institute for Visual History and Education project in the 1990s. I was one of tens of thousands from over 50 countries that volunteered to archive my Holocaust story.

Philanthropist Lois Lehrman Grass, a wonderful person and friend, approached me to create an educational endowment foundation. We call it *Gesher L'Machar*, or "Bridge to Tomorrow." The program supports local teenagers who wish to participate in the March of the Living, an annual trip to Poland and Israel to study the Holocaust.

Education was very important. When I was in high school, I wrote a paper on what freedom meant to me. I had it in my mind that I wanted to see schools in Central Pennsylvania research the Holocaust. I formed a foundation and now give 2 thousand dollars in cash to the winners from junior and senior high. The local newspaper, *The Patriot-News*, helped publicize the project. The winner of the essay contest is expected to read his or her essay on *Yom Hashoah*, the Holocaust Memorial Day, at the Holocaust monument in Harrisburg.

I am very most proud of this next project. I consider it to be the capstone project. Morrie and I created the Schwab Family Holocaust Reading Room located in the library at Penn State University-Harrisburg. The reading room is the cornerstone of the college's Holocaust and Jewish Studies Center. In it are hundreds of resources related to the Holocaust. Included among the documents are stories of local Holocaust survivors. This is where I will eventually store all of my memorabilia.

Unfortunately, Morrie passed away on December 19, 2006, a few months before the reading room was dedicated. The reading room is just as much his legacy as it is mine.

I asked for 10 good years. He gave me 23 wonderful years. I adored him, and he adored me.

CHAPTER 24

MY BROTHER, HAROLD, remembers a lot more than I do, especially in the language department. For instance, I think to this day, he speaks Russian and Hebrew much better than I do. However, my youngest brother, Norman, remembers very little about our experience during the war.

Though I have never returned to Myadel, Harold and his wife Eileen did after the collapse of the Soviet Union, and, as my family refers to it, "the Iron Curtain was lifted" in the early '90s.

They were very active in Jewish uplift in their hometown of Carlisle, Pennsylvania. They sponsored the Israeli soldiers that came to the War College. They once met a colonel from Belarus, who encouraged Harold to visit his old home. When landed in Myadel, Harold had difficulty recognizing anything until he met the only Jewish person in the village, Mones Gorden. Mones remembered Harold. He showed Harold where our house was. He tried to show Harold where we hid out. While on a dirt road, they encountered a farmer. They asked the farmer who they could speak with that might remember our father. According to my brother's account, the man exclaimed, "I know about Hendele." He said, "If you don't believe me, I will take you to see my father-in-law, and he will tell you about Hendele." The man's father-in-law was Alexander!

Alexander told Harold and Eileen all about how he helped to save us during the war. Harold left him everything he had on him and called me in the middle of the night to tell me he fund Alexander. You have to know, Alexander is the only name we remember.

When my granddaughter, Alie, was *Bat Mitzahed*, I didn't want her to stop her Jewish education, so I promised her that I would take her on the March of the Living if she continued through Hebrew High. She was excited about that.

When my granddaughter Lauren, heard about the proposition, she insisted on going too. I told her I would make it happen. Lauren was a senior in high school, and she had to be prepared. So, we joined the District of Columbia's *B'nai B'rith* Youth Organization (BBYO), a youth chapter of a national organization for young Jewish boys and girls. The BBYO is also known as the world's leading Jewish youth group dedicated to leadership training, community service, and global Jewish consciousness. *B'nai B'rith* is Hebrew for "Sons of the covenant," which was founded on October 13, 1843. It is the oldest Jewish organization in American history. Considering that it was founded during Antebellum, it is perhaps among the oldest and longest-lasting national organizations in the country. Its Youth Organization was established to promote the loyalty of Jewish religious values and educate students through programs designed to counteract prejudice and discrimination. This is the institution that prepared Lauren for the journey to Israel.

It was an unbelievable trip for Lauren and me. This was the first time back in Poland. During the trip, I told my story to the entire group, and the kids and the adults were sitting there with their mouths wide open. Though I had the impression that they had heard stories of the concentration camps, it appeared that they knew nothing about how people survived in the forest. I was treated as though I was royalty. They wanted to sit with me. Everyone insisted on having Shabbat with me. They wanted to ask me questions. We developed very close bonds.

It was heartwarming for me to see these young adults walking through the crematoriums learning about their heritage and learning about what happened in the death camps. I think those children will never forget what happened during the Holocaust.

When we were traveling to the different concentration camps, and I saw the forests, those dense woods, those trees, it reminded me when I hid out as a young child. Though I don't cry anymore, I had flashbacks and felt empty inside. The following week we arrived in Israel Tel Aviv. My granddaughter, Lauren, and I visited my cousins, whose apartment building was right next to the Israel legislature, the Knesset. Their grandparents were also killed in the Holocaust. Their mother was Shura, who had survived the Dachau concentration camp and eventually connected with us at the Fohrenwald DP Camp with her sister, Frieda. We spent the time in Israel learning about a young country during its Independence Day celebration.

On the trip, Lauren and I bonded. I know she will continue to educate her peers about the trip, which she expressed to me was her favorite life experience.

I was exhausted when I returned home. Reliving my Holocaust experience was emotionally draining. My immune system was so weak that I came down with a terrible cold. It took about three weeks to get back on my feet. Despite the hardship, it was worth knowing that this Holocaust will not be forgotten. After all, the March of the Living aims to spread awareness so that the next generation will carry on the memory of the Holocaust to that this atrocity will not be forgotten.

I was good to my promise. And when Ali was a senior, I took her on the March of the Living. She was every bit as excited about the trip as Lauren had been years earlier. When we arrived at the Warsaw airport, I noticed a familiar-looking woman breeze by me. I approached her to ask where she was from. She said, Los Angeles.

I shook my head and said, "What is your name?"

"Paula," she replied.

The bells went off in my head. I screamed, "You're not Paula. You are Pese."

She retorted, "How do you know me?"

"I'm Lile, from the DP Camp."

A few times, we visited one another. We email each other often now.

When it was my granddaughter Caroline's turn, I kept the promise to her. We went on the March of the Living with BBYO for my third time. My daughter Sandee and her friend, Lisa Riner, joined us.

I took Sandee and my granddaughter, Caroline, on the March of the Living in the fall of 2015. We first traveled to Poland, where we toured the remnants of the camp at Majdanek. At a scale of horror that nearly compares to Auschwitz, Majdenek detained the largest number of children (5,000) that were labor and as blood bank depositors. Older Jewish prisoners at Majdenek were forced to flatten the mass graves of Soviet POWs that had died before Jews were transited there. Most Jews arrived there from the Czech and Slovakian territories. In just three months' time, when construction began on March 25, 1942 to June 1942, the camp was filled with over 15,000 prisoners. Almost all were Jewish. Men, women, and children were placed into separate camps. For most of its existence, Majdanek was used as a labor camp. Of course, the camp's earliest prisoners died of malnutrition, overwork, and exposure to extremely cold temperatures. In October 1942, however, a gas chamber was constructed. From that point onward, Zyklon B and carbon monoxide were used to kill new arrivals to Majdanek. About 16,000 were killed in the first year after the gas chamber was built. The ashes of the cremated bodies were scattered in the Krepiecki forest. There was a huge monument at the entrance of the camp. It was a place where ash remains were kept.

Warsaw is near Majdenek. So Sandee, Caroline, and I took an excursion to Poland's capital city to tour the Warsaw ghetto and seminary. Together, we walked through the hallowed ground in silence. We learned about the mass deportations in freight cars from the Warsaw ghetto beginning in 1942 to various death camps throughout Poland, and how those mass deportations eventually inspired those trapped in the ghetto to fight back on April 19, 1943. The Warsaw ghetto uprising is an inspiring story where Jewish resisters stood up to their killers by attacking German soldiers with Molotov cocktails and guns that had been smuggled into the ghetto by partisans.

We then caught a plane from Warsaw to Israel, where I was determined to track down the children and grandchildren of my late-cousin, Lile, who, with me, had survived those harsh conditions in the Zimlanke for almost two years. We arrived in Tel Aviv on a Friday night but needed to get to Nazareth and then Haifa, where we believed Lile's daughter and son, Smadar and Near, lived. So we chose to get some sleep and begin our journey in the morning. The problem was, we would start our adventure on the Sabbath. This meant Israeli public transit was closed. So the three of us hired an Arab taxi. Our driver only spoke Arabic, so he brought along his wife and daughter, who did speak English and could thus serve as a translator while on the journey to Haifa, along the Black Sea. We arrived at the only address I had in my notes for Lile's family, which took us to an apartment complex. We knocked on seven different doors. Each time the people inside would open the door just a crack to peek out at us. And each said they didn't know Yiddish or English before slamming the door in our faces.

When we knocked on the eighth door, an elderly lady actually came outside to talk with us. I asked her in Yiddish, "Do you speak Yiddish?"

"Certainly," she answered.

"How long have you lived here."

She replied, "A long time. How can I help you?

I asked, "Do you know my Aunt Henya?"

"Yes. She died years ago."

"So then you knew my cousin, Lile?"

"Yes. She died too."

"I am aware of that," I said. "But do you know where Lile's children are living?"

"Well, they moved away."

At that moment, one of the women who previously slammed a door in my face came outside. She had been listening to my queries through her door. I never asked her name, but she said to me: "I knew your family." Then she gave me a phone book with a page marked. It had the number of a young man who was friends with Smadar. I called him on my cell phone. Curious at first, this individual ultimately helped us track down Near and Smadar in a suburb called Neva Shanan, located along with the ranges of Mount Carmel, known to locals as "the balcony of the country," about 20 miles away from Haifa.

I felt like a detective, and my mission to find my relatives was almost accomplished. All that was left was a bus ride to the foot of the mountain, where Near and Smadar, along with her daughter Hila, said they would meet us. The bus driver had a hard time finding the house, but eventually, I saw the address on the side of an apartment building. I yelled out, "Stop!" The driver said he couldn't turn the bus around. He pulled over to the side of the road. I hurried out and called Smadar on the phone. She told me to stay there, and she'd be run to my location to pick me up.

I couldn't control my emotions when I saw Smadar and Hila running toward me. My knees were shaking. I felt like I was going to faint. My daughter Sandee had to hold me up. It was a very emotional moment for all of us. We didn't stop hugging one another for several minutes. Spending time with them was one of the highlights of my life. As you can image, because of the suffering Lile and I faced during World War II, I wanted to be just as close with her child and grandchild as I was with her. Before we parted, I reached into my pocketbook and gave her all the money I had. I insisted she share it with her family.

I would see Smader and Hila once again when I took my oldest granddaughter, Erica, on a trip to Poland and Israel in October 2018. I guess you can say that I arranged an informal March of the Living excursion, as I showed Erica most of the Holocaust landmarks that the international tour traditionally visits. We traveled through Poland before arriving in Israel to visit with my relatives. Regrettably, my cousin Near had passed away, but our visit with Smadar and Hila was extraordinary. Erica was able to see all the same places that I visited on my 2015 March of the Living trip. This time, we went at our leisure and stayed in nice hotels. I was not as tired by the end of the journey. We had Smadar and Hila at our hotel and spent time with them, which was very important for me.

Sandee and I took pleasure in having Erica tag along. We bonded and showed her places we had never been to before. We visited with each of the families so that Erica would get to know them better. Since that trip was probably the last time that I will travel to Israel, I hired a private guide with his own vehicle, who proved to possess a wealth of knowledge. After all, I'm over 80 but not in bad shape. I want to stay well.

Since Morrie's passing, I am still in Florida for the winters playing golf and bridge, while spending time with friends and family. I still go to *shul*, or synagogue, on the High Holidays. I belong to two temples, and I continue to speak at schools where I am needed.

While writing this memoir, my brother, Harold, found a recording of Pop being interviewed by Morrie's son, Jim. The interview was conducted about five years after we came to the United States, long before Morrie and I were married. I learned all the questions that I wished I had asked before he passed away. I heard my father's voice in his broken English. I cried. I played it on repeat over and over. This tape had been in Harold's nightstand all these years, and he never knew what it was.

I spoke to a group of students and friends in 2016 at Penn State University-Harrisburg. The event was standing room only. The professor that introduced me, Anthony Buccitelli, also the director of the Center for Holocaust and Jewish Studies at the university, called me afterward. "I have a doctoral student who is very interested in writing your story," he said. "I gave him your email, hope that's all right with you." The student was Todd Mealy, who now has his Ph.D. and is co-authoring this memoir. Now that it is finished, I feel relieved.

I know my children, grandchildren, and great-grandchildren, and all of you will know Linda Schwab's story. I hope readers will continue to tell it, so the past will never be forgotten.

I feel strongly that God saved me so I can tell the world how I survived.

When asked to give a public lecture to a class or at a university, I always finish with the same statement: "I come to tell you my story because I want you to be my ambassadors for when I'm gone. So you can respond to deniers that claim the Holocaust never happened. You will be able to say, 'Yes, it did. Have you met Linda Schwab?'"

ABOUT THE AUTHORS

LINDA SWIDLER was born December 1935 in Myadel, Poland (present-day Belarus). The Nazis invaded her shtetl in 1942. After witnessing the killing of the people from her village, the Swidlers went into hiding in the Ponar Forest. With the help of people in the nearby village, Linda and her family survived in cave-like conditions until the end of World War II. After the war, Linda lived in the Fohrenwald Displaced Persons Camp located in Bavaria, Germany. She and her family arrived in the United States in 1949. After decades of silence, she finally opened up about her Holocaust experience in the early 1990s as a participant in Steven Spielberg's Shoah Foundation Institute for History and Education. Linda now tells her story to K-12 and post-secondary students. She is cofounder of *Gesher L'Machar*, or "Bridge to Tomorrow," which sponsors students who wish to participate in the annual Holocaust trip to Poland and Israel called The March of the Living. Linda also sponsors a Holocaust Memorial Day essay contest. Named in honor of Linda and her late husband, Morris, is The Schwab Family Holocaust Reading Room at Penn State University-Harrisburg.

TODD M. MEALY is a contributing writer at *Pennsylvania Heritage* and the author of six books. With a Ph.D. in American Studies from Pennsylvania State University-Harrisburg, he is the Director of Equity and Instruction for The Bond Educational Group, where he also leads The Equity Institute for Race Conscious Pedagogy. An educator of almost two decades, including tenures in K-12 and higher education, Mealy's scholarship has concentrated on 19th and 20th century civil rights history and critical race studies in the 21st century.

Made in the USA
Middletown, DE
12 October 2023

40711941R00076